CU00701248

The J(

Wedding

and the

Bride of Christ

by

Mo Tizzard

STOREHOUSE BOOKS

EASTBOURNE

STOREHOUSE
BOOKS

Unless otherwise indicated, biblical quotations are from the New International Version © 1973, 1978, 1984 by the International Bible Society (Italics added for emphasis)
Biblical quotations marked (NKJV) are from the New King James Version (c) 1982 by Thomas Nelson, Inc. Used by permission. All rights reserved. (Italics added for emphasis)

ISBN – 978-0-9566249-1-8

Published by
STOREHOUSE BOOKS
19 Trossachs Close, Eastbourne,
BN23 8HA, England
Email: storehousebooks@sky.com

Cover Design by Jonathan Stanbrook
www.jonathanstanbrook.co.uk

www.motizzard.com

Acknowledgements

Many thanks go to all those who have encouraged me to put this teaching into a book, especially Karen Way and the staff and students training with Youth With A Mission's Urban DTS in Derby.

I also want to thank my dear friends Anne Veasey, Corinne Ayres and Elizabeth Beeney. In using their different skills they have been such a help to me with proof reading, encouragement and prayer.

Much love goes to my bridegroom, Bill who married this bride more than forty years ago.

Finally many blessings and love go to my mum, who met the Matchmaker and said 'Yes' to our Bridegroom earlier this year at the tender age of ninety years old! It's never too late!

Contents

	Introduction	5
	An Encouragement from the Author	8
1.	The Jewish Wedding	10
	Arranged Marriages	11
2.	The First Stage of the Wedding	16
	The Matchmaker	20
3.	The Contract	24
4.	The Bride Price	30
5.	The Dowry	36
6.	Ceremonial Cleansing	42
7.	The Second Stage of the Wedding	48
	The Betrothal Ceremony	49
8.	The Cup	56
9.	The Ring	62
10.	The Blessing	68
11.	After the Ceremony	74
12.	The Gifts	80
13.	The Groom's Preparation	87
14.	The Bride's Preparation	92
15.	Waiting for the Bridegroom	98
16.	The Return of the Bridegroom	105
17.	The Bridal Garments	110
18.	The Third Stage of the Wedding	118
19.	The Wedding Supper	125
20.	The Consummation	130

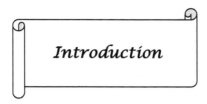

Introduction

There is nothing more beautiful than the sight of a bride dressed in all her finery, walking down the aisle towards her waiting groom, on their wedding day. But for joy, there is nothing to rival the look on the face of the groom when he sees her coming. As she gets nearer and nearer he only has eyes for her. He isn't looking at the congregation or her bridesmaids; he isn't looking at his friends acting as groomsmen or ushers. He only has eyes for the woman he loves.

In this book I want to try to give some understanding that you, personally, are in that amazing and privileged position of being the one who is being looked upon with such love and devotion; that you have been chosen by Jesus to share His life for eternity. You are the central figure with Him, in this wonderful scenario, in this wedding arranged by our Father and His. You are not just a part of the wedding, you are not 'always the bridesmaid' - you are His Bride!

'For I have betrothed you to one husband, to Christ, so that I might present you as a pure virgin to him.' 2 Corinthians 11:2

It's interesting to note that the actual phrase 'the bride of Christ' isn't found in the Bible. But the apostle Paul makes it clear in the above scripture that we are betrothed to Christ; and if we are betrothed to Him then we are indeed His bride.

The word 'betrothed' is the Greek word *harmozo*. I should imagine this is where we get our English word for harmony. Because the word *harmozo* not only means 'to betroth', but it also means 'to join', 'to fit together', as when a carpenter fastens beams and planks together to build a house or a ship, etc. What a wonderful picture this brings to mind of our being joined together with Jesus, our Bridegroom in order to make a house, a home that many new believers can be born into!

As I have looked into the stages of the Jewish wedding, not as it is conducted today, but as it was conducted in the culture when both the Old and New Testaments were written, I've been thrilled to discover that there is such a correlation between the Jewish wedding and ours, as the betrothed bride of Christ, with Jesus our Bridegroom. I would like to share with you what I have found and I think you'll be surprised, and I hope amazed and thrilled too, at how the individual stages and the elements of this wedding relate to us now.

It is my prayer that you will see and understand all the fullness of what the Lord has promised to us, His betrothed bride. That despite the fact that the covenant He made with us was written thousands of years ago, it hasn't changed - even though the world around us has.

An Encouragement from the Author

Before you begin I'd like to encourage you to take your time and allow the teaching in this book to sink in. I know that when I'm reading something new or something I've forgotten about, I'm always eager to move on to the next chapter, to discover what else is to come. I guess you could say I get hungry for more. But as you read this book can I persuade you to take what I call a 'Selah' break between the chapters. We often read the word Selah at the end of the lines in many of the Psalms. The word means 'to lift up, to exalt'. It was inserted to tell the singers that they should stop singing at this point and listen to the music. Selah is from the word *sala*, which means to value and weigh. As a young Christian I was told that Selah meant, 'stop and think on these things', which is very close to the true meaning of the word.

There's a lot in this book that I'm sure will give you the desire 'to lift up, to exalt' our wonderful Saviour; and much that will enlighten your understanding as you see things through different cultural eyes. That being so, I would recommend that if you can stop and think about each chapter, 'chew' on what you've read for a while, before moving on, you will get more out of it, and it will add to your enjoyment of the book as a whole.

Therefore I am giving you a blank page at the end of each chapter so that you can write down your thoughts, your observations and any fresh insights that He will give you personally. Or you might want to illustrate your thoughts rather than write them down, or maybe a mixture of both. If you don't have enough room on the one page, you will find there is often a space at the end of the chapter that you could use too. If you are a Kindle reader then maybe you could use a notebook instead. Of course you may want to read it all through first and then come back and read it for a second time slowly and then do the Selah pages. Catherine Butcher, who did the review for the back cover decided to do that, because as she said, "I didn't want to put it down". But of course you may not want to do the Selah pages at all. But whatever you do decide I pray that you'll enjoy all the elements that the Jewish wedding and our wedding to the King of kings entails.

Many blessings,

Mo

Chapter One

The Jewish Wedding

In biblical times there were three stages to the Jewish Wedding. The first stage was the arrangement period or the *Shidduchin*. The second stage was the betrothal period or the *Kiddushin*, which in Hebrew means 'sanctification' or 'set apart'. The third and final stage of the wedding was the *Nissuin*, meaning 'elevation'. This final stage lifted them to the status of being man and wife in every sense of the word. In modern times the arrangement stage of the wedding has been dropped, leaving it to the couples themselves to decide; and the other two stages, the *Kiddushin* and the *Nissuin*, are combined with both ceremonies being performed together on the same day.

Arranged Marriages

Long ago arranged marriages were normal, understood and expected in many countries; and in some places it is still a part of their life and culture, even to the present day. But an arranged marriage is not something that those of us who are from a Western culture know much about.

Marriage wasn't taken lightly and love did not come into it, unlike most modern marriages today, although it could be a secondary issue. Parents wanted their children to make good marriages and the children weren't deemed wise enough to know what that involved. So the parents took it as their responsibility to make sure that their son or daughter married into a good family. Marriage was an important opportunity for a high born family to make good connections with other high born families. The right marriage was also vital in making good political alliances. It was often used as a means to bring peace, or to strengthen the alliance between two countries, by joining their royal houses together through marriage. In these cases, it would involve the bride leaving her own country to marry and live in the groom's home and country, which could be a long distance away. In the days when travel was long and often difficult, this could mean that the intended couple didn't meet each other until just before the wedding, or even on the wedding day itself!

But arranged marriages didn't just take place in royal, political or high born families. Even in poorer households, parents considered it their duty to make sure their children married into good families; that the marriage they arranged for them would give them the best possible advantage in life.

The couple's feelings were not relevant the most important thing was to obtain the best match possible for everyone's sake. That was because their children were not just being joined to one person, they were being joined to that person's whole family! The parents of the potential bride were very aware that their daughter would be leaving their family and becoming part of the groom's family. It was vital therefore that she was married to someone who belonged to a good, respectable family, because their daughter would be involved in all the aspects of his family's life. She would be expected to do many of the family's household tasks - under the supervision of her mother-in-law of course. Also, depending on the size of the household and the number of hired hands, she may be required to help out in the fields, especially at harvest time. Then, when his parents became too old to work, and her mother-in-law was too old to do the household tasks, she would be expected to take them over. Added to this she would be responsible for taking care of his elderly parents in their old age, and look after their welfare.

Therefore her family would need to know that this was a family they could trust their daughter with because the intended husband was only one part of the whole package.

Where marriage was concerned, the choice of the groom would be considered and the consent of the bride was usual, but the consideration of a good family and good connections were much more important than whether the bride and groom loved each other, as they are in our modern world today.

'Then Naomi said to her two daughters–in-law, "Go back, each of you, to your mother's home. May the LORD show kindness to you, as you have shown to your dead and to me. May the LORD grant that each of you will find rest in the home of another husband" Then she kissed them and they wept aloud and said to her, "We will go back with you to your people." But Naomi said, "Return home, my daughters...."' Ruth 1:8-11a

The best way to illustrate what marriage meant for the bride, in leaving her family to live with her husband's family, is to look at the story of Ruth. Naomi and her husband Elimelech left Israel when there was a famine in the land, and they moved to Moab. With them were their two sons Mahlon and Chilion. After some time Elimelech died and, as there were no suitable Israelite families to arrange a marriage with, both the sons married Moabite women. Mahlon, who was probably the eldest as he is listed first, married Ruth; and Chilion married Orpah.

After ten years of marriage, both Mahlon and Chilion died and the three women were left on their own without husbands, or in Naomi's case, sons to support them. In those days there weren't any jobs for women apart from prostitution. A woman's life revolved around her family and her housekeeping duties. So without her sons to work and provide for them Naomi knew she had to return home to Bethlehem in the territory of Judah. She had to return to the only family she had left, and they were still living in Israel.

When Ruth or Orpah had married their husbands they had married into their family, this was their family forever. Therefore it was Naomi who had to tell them to return to their 'mother's home', rather than stay with their mother-in-law. Naomi could not bear any more sons who could marry them and provide for them according to the custom of the time where a widow married the brother of her dead husband (see Deuteronomy 25:5). If they returned to their Moabite family homes their fathers could then arrange a second marriage for them and secure their futures, 'The LORD grant, that you will find rest in the home of another husband' (Ruth 1:9).

Orpah, with great sadness, decided to leave her mother-in-law and return to her parent's home. But Ruth decided to stay with Naomi. She not only loved her mother-in-law but she realised that Naomi was too old to make that journey alone and she considered it her duty to take care of her in her old age, as any daughter-in-law would do. Ruth still considered herself part of her husband's family - even though it didn't include him!

Chapter Two

The First Stage of the Wedding

A mate was often chosen for the child while he or she was still an infant, but not always. The father was the person responsible to find a suitable mate for his child, but sometimes he used a representative instead. That person was called a matchmaker.

If you've ever seen the musical 'Fiddler on the Roof' I'm sure you'll remember the scene where the girls of the family are sweeping the house while dancing and singing, "Matchmaker, matchmaker, make me a match, find me a find, catch me a catch". In the production the matchmaker was an elderly lady who was given the task of finding suitable husbands and wives for the children of the families in that village. This was the usual way that marriages in Russia, and Eastern Europe were arranged at the time in which the musical was set, which was around the beginning of the twentieth century. The musical aims to show how the Jewish people carried on their traditions then; and some of those traditions dated back to the time of the Patriarchs, including arranged marriages.

In Genesis 24 we read that Abraham entrusted the task of matchmaker to his oldest and most trustworthy servant. The servant was to go to the area where Abraham's relatives lived to find a suitable bride for his son Isaac.

'Now Abraham was old, well advanced in age; and the LORD had blessed Abraham in all things.

So Abraham said to the oldest servant of his house, who ruled over all that he had, "Please, put your hand under my thigh, and I will make you swear by the LORD, the God of heaven and the God of the earth, that you will not take a wife for my son from the daughters of the Canaanites, among whom I dwell; but you shall go to my country and to my family, and take a wife for my son Isaac."

And the servant said to him, "Perhaps the woman will not be willing to follow me to this land. Must I take your son back to the land from which you came?" But Abraham said to him, "Beware that you do not take my son back there. The LORD God of heaven, who took me from my father's house and from the land of my family, and who spoke to me and swore to me, saying, 'To your descendants I give this land,' He will send His angel before you, and you shall take a wife for my son from there.

And if the woman is not willing to follow you, then you will be released from this oath; only do not take my son back there."

So the servant put his hand under the thigh of Abraham his master, and swore to him concerning this matter.

Then the servant took ten of his master's camels and departed, for all his master's goods were in his hand. And he arose and went to Mesopotamia, to the city of Nahor.'
Genesis 24:1-10 (NKJV)

Putting his hand under Abraham's thigh (v.9) was an ancient custom that indicated the servant was undertaking a very serious oath. The thigh is the strongest part of the body, so the oath being taken was to be a strong oath. Also, according to the concordance, the thigh is indicative of the loins, as the seat of procreative power, and it was for procreative purposes that the servant was to be sent on his mission. He was to find a good wife, of the right stock for Isaac who would ensure the continuation of Abraham's line.

The need for the strong oath was so that Abraham could have complete assurance that his wishes would be followed to the letter. That was because if Abraham died while the servant was still away on his mission, Abraham would have had no recourse to revoke any wrong decisions. The servant was made to swear that he would not find a wife for Isaac locally among the Canaanites, who worshipped idols. He was to find a bride from among his relatives. If the potential bride could not be persuaded to return with him, the servant

had to swear that he would not take Isaac back to that land
in order to persuade her - 'do not take my son back there'.

The potential bride was to accept the servant's proposal
without seeing Isaac, the son, or even having proof that he
existed. If she refused to return with him then his duty was
discharged and the servant was free from his obligation to
Abraham. This was agreed and the servant was sent a long
distance to the area where Abraham's relatives lived.

'Then he prayed, "O LORD, God of my master Abraham,
give me success this day, and show kindness to my master,
Abraham. See, I am standing beside this spring, and the
daughters of the townspeople are coming out to draw water.
May it be that when I say to a girl, 'Please let down your jar
that I may have a drink,' and she says, 'Drink, and I'll water
your camels too' – let her be the one you have chosen for
your servant Isaac. By this I will know that you have shown
kindness to my master."
Before he had finished praying, Rebekah came out with her
jar on her shoulder. She was the daughter of Bethuel son of
Milcah, who was the wife of Abraham's brother Nahor.'
Genesis 24:12-15

The servant's prayer was answered immediately and he met
Rebekah, who was the granddaughter of Abraham's brother
Nahor. She was also the sister of Laban, who years later was
to became Jacob's father-in-law. Rebekah's family were very
positive about her leaving them to become Isaac's bride. But

before they finally agreed they asked her what she felt about it. Was she happy to leave her family and go with Abraham's servant in order to marry his son? Her parents may have wanted the marriage to go ahead, but the final decision was hers – 'Let's call the girl and ask her about it. So they called Rebekah and asked her, "Will you go with this man?"' (Genesis 24:58). Happily Rebekah agreed to return with Abraham's servant to be Isaac's bride - even though she had never met him!

The Matchmaker

The name of the matchmaker, who was Abraham's eldest and most trustworthy servant, was Eliezer (see Genesis 15:2). The name Eliezer means 'God is my help'.

"I will pray the Father and He will give you another Helper, that He may abide with you forever – the Spirit of truth." John 14:16 (NKJV)

The name Eliezer, 'God is my help', brings to mind the last supper that Jesus had with His disciples. During that time, before He was about to be arrested and crucified, He shared the most important things that they would need to know. This included the news that when He returned to heaven He would send another 'Helper' to be with them forever - the Holy Spirit.

The word used for 'helper' or 'counsellor' as it is sometimes translated, is the Greek word *parakletos*. A *parakletos* is described as a counsellor, a comforter, or an advocate; one who assists in giving help or relief. The best summary of all these attributes that I've heard is, 'one who comes alongside' to help in all circumstances and situations.

The news that the disciples would be sent another Helper, the Holy Spirit who would help them and counsel them, was just part of the story. The Holy Spirit was also sent as the Father's Helper - the Father's Matchmaker. Like Abraham's servant, Eliezer, the Holy Spirit has been sent a 'long distance' by the Father and He has been entrusted to find a bride for His Son. It is the Holy Matchmaker's job to persuade all those who will listen to Him, to accept the offer from the Father, to be joined to His Son and become a member of His family. It is our heavenly Father's desire that all would respond to this wonderful offer, but like Rebekah, it's up to us, each individual, to accept His proposal, agree to leave our old life and go with the Father's Matchmaker, the Father's Helper, to be the Son's bride. But our decision can only be based on 'faith, not sight' (2 Cor. 5:7), because the Son will not leave the place He has with His Father in heaven to come and find a bride for Himself. He is staying with His Father waiting for those who are willing to come to Him and be completely His – forever!

'Though you have not seen him, you love him; and even though you do not see him now, you believe in him and are filled with an inexpressible and glorious joy, for you are receiving the goal of your faith, the salvation of your souls.' 1 Peter 1:8

This picture of the Father sending the Holy Matchmaker to seek us out to be the Son's bride makes something else very clear. Jesus said to His disciples at the Last Supper - "You did not choose me, but I chose you" John 15:16.

Chapter Three

The Contract

The next step in the arrangement period, or *Shidduchin*, was the formation of a marriage contract or marriage covenant, called the *Ketubah*. The name comes from the Hebrew word *katav*, which means 'to write'. The contract or *Ketubah* was a written document, which the intended groom prepared and presented to the young woman's father stating what would be included in the marriage. This had to be acceptable to both parties before the contract was agreed to and the planned marriage could go ahead.

This contract wasn't the same as a present day pre-nuptial agreement, where the parties involved draw up an agreement to make sure their assets are protected, if the marriage fails and they end up in the divorce courts. It wasn't a contract designed to save them a lot of money through long drawn out court battles. Although divorce was possible in days gone by as a result of adultery, or due to the hardness of men's hearts (see Matthew 19:8), this didn't often happen because they took covenants or contracts very seriously then.

It's not easy for us today to understand the strength of a contract in the way that they would view it. Most contracts these days are 'not worth the paper they are written on'. Footballers and managers are the most obvious example of the modern day contract. They mean very little when more money or prestige is offered to a footballer by another football club; or if a manager doesn't live up to expectations and doesn't 'deliver the goods' by making sure his team wins regularly. People nowadays don't have any problem in just tearing up a contract and signing a new one. The most heartbreaking situations these days are when marriage contracts are treated in the same way. When adultery takes place or when one or both partners don't live up to expectations.

God knows the heartache that comes through the breaking of a contract. He delivered the Old Covenant to Moses on Mount Sinai, who then presented it to the people of Israel. They said, "Everything the LORD has said we will do." (Exodus 24:3 & 24:7). They agreed to abide by the terms of what we call the Old Covenant, or contract that the LORD had drawn up. You may well ask what has this to do with a marriage contract. Well in Ezekiel 16:32 we read of the LORD saying to His people, "You adulterous wife!" and in

Jeremiah 31:32 He says, ".... they broke my covenant though I was a husband to them". It seems from these scriptures, and from others, that the LORD considered the covenant made between Himself and His people, was like a marriage contract. Because when they turned away from being devoted to Him in order to worship idols, He saw this in the context of their breaking a contract or covenant in the same way that an unfaithful wife would.

But although they had broken the Old Covenant by being unfaithful, the LORD didn't 'wash His hands' of His chosen people. Through the prophet Jeremiah the LORD gives them hope for the future when He says:

"The time is coming when I will make a new covenant with the house of Israel and the house of Judah"" Jeremiah 31:31.

This isn't just a new covenant, a new marriage contract for the Israelites alone. This is a contract offered to all of us. Because the next few verses go on to tell us how this covenant will operate.

"This is the covenant I will make with the house of Israel after that time," declares the LORD. "I will put my law in their minds and write it on their hearts. I will be their God, and they will be my people.
No longer will a man teach his neighbour, or a man his brother, saying 'Know the LORD', because they will all know

me, from the least of them to the greatest" declares the
LORD.
"For I will forgive their wickedness and will remember their
sins no more.'" Jeremiah 31:33-34

The Old Covenant Law was first written on stone and then
on parchment. But because the majority of people couldn't
read in those days, it was read and taught to the people by
the teachers of the Law. However, it is impossible for man
to keep all the instructions included in a contract as stringent
as the Old Testament Law, because the Law, as God's first
representative on earth, is perfect and man isn't. The Law
just shows us how weak we are and how much we need a
Saviour.

So through Jeremiah, the LORD made it clear that one day
when the New Covenant came, the teachers of the Law
would no longer be needed – 'no longer will a man teach his
neighbour, or a man his brother'. Instead each man, woman
and child, from any walk of life, would be able to know the
LORD, because He will put His law in their minds and write
it on their hearts. Those who receive His New Covenant are
promised that they will not only receive knowledge of the
Lord, His character and His ways, but also knowledge of
how to act and react in ways that please Him. This
knowledge is imparted direct from His Holy Spirit into our
spirits and is freely available to all, not just the people that
Jeremiah originally spoke to. It's for both Jew and Gentile, it
encompasses all peoples and all nations.

The New Covenant, the new marriage contract, the new Ketubah, was prepared, presented and delivered by our Bridegroom to the Father of us all. It was perfectly acceptable to the Father and the Son; and as we go through all that was involved, and included in the Jewish Wedding in the time of both the Old and New Covenants, I think you will begin to see more clearly how acceptable it is to us.

'For this reason Christ is the mediator of a *new covenant*, that those who are called may receive the promised eternal inheritance....' Hebrews 9:15

'Selah'

Chapter Four

The Bride Price

Included in the marriage contract or covenant was the bride price, called the *Mohar*. This was appropriate in that society to compensate the bride's parents for the cost of raising her. Because every member of a family was required to be involved in making their family income work, to give a daughter away in marriage meant the loss of a productive worker around the house and on the land. So the bride price was required by her parents to make up for that loss. However in some cases, the bride price could also be an expression of the groom's love for his bride.

Jacob was prepared to pay a bride price of seven years of hard work to Laban in order to marry Laban's younger daughter Rachel, who we are told was 'beautiful of form and appearance' (see Genesis 29:17-18). Although seven years seems a lot to us, it seemed quite fair and reasonable to

Jacob. He was so besotted with the lovely Rachel that he probably thought she was worth 'a million dollars'; and he would probably have agreed to anything just to marry her!

Jacob served seven years for Rachel, and we are told that they 'seemed only a few days to him because of his love for her.' (Genesis 29:20). However, when he had completed his seven years of work, poor Jacob was tricked by Laban into sleeping with his eldest daughter on his wedding night. Laban substituted Rachel for her elder sister Leah by covering Leah with a heavy veil and taking her to Jacob's tent. Because it was dark and the virginal bride would have probably been shy and embarrassed, Jacob was unaware he was sleeping with the wrong sister until daylight dawned. Then there was nothing Jacob could do, because once you had slept with a woman you were duty bound to marry her. In fact the wedding night was the marriage ceremony in Jacob's day. Laban tricked Jacob in this way because according to him, and maybe to custom, it was important and appropriate that the eldest daughter was married first. But the way Laban managed it wasn't appropriate at all!

The outcome of that trickery meant that Jacob's seven years of work, dedicated to his lovely Rachel, was taken by Laban as the bride price for his marrying Leah - even though she wasn't part of the agreement. But having slept with her, she was now his wife. So Jacob couldn't do anything about it, other than agree to work another seven years in order to earn another bride price, so that he could marry his beloved

Rachel. But this time Jacob insisted the bride price would be paid for in hindsight; and one week after his marriage to Leah he finally fulfilled his heart's desire and married Rachel.

Whenever I read this story I feel really sorry for poor Leah. During the seven years that had elapsed since Jacob first declared his love for Rachel, it seems that no-one had been willing to pay a bride price for her hand in marriage. Plus on top of that Jacob had worked for fourteen years and paid two bride prices - and both of them were for Rachel! He didn't even work one day for Leah's hand in marriage. It seems she wasn't worth anyone's bride price; she could only get a husband by her father's trickery – how humiliating. However, God made up for that and recompensed her later on. But that's for another book!

We have a Suitor who loved us enough to pay a huge bride price for us. Fourteen years of hard work seems nothing in the light of how much our Bridegroom was willing to pay for our hand in marriage. The bride price that He paid for us to be His bride can be found written in the New Testament, but it was decided, prophesied and written down centuries before, by Isaiah in the Old Testament.

'For thus says the LORD: "You were sold for nothing, and *without money* you will be redeemed"' Isaiah 52:3

To redeem something, means that a price has been paid, to transfer something or someone from one owner to another;

'And Laban gave his servant girl Zilpah to his daughter Leah as her maidservant.... Laban gave his servant girl Bilhah to his daughter Rachel as her maidservant.' Genesis 29:24 & 29

In Ruth chapter three we read that Boaz agrees to act on behalf of Ruth & Naomi in order to find them a kinsman redeemer. One who would purchase the land belonging to Naomi's family and marry Ruth, according to the law for the provision of widows and the perpetuation of a dead man's inheritance (see Deuteronomy 25:5). Naomi wasn't able to sell the land and arrange Ruth's marriage herself because both came under the heading of business - and women weren't legally allowed to conduct business. It had to be done by men and witnessed by ten elders of the city. Therefore, Boaz agrees to take on this business matter for them, to represent their interests, and if necessary be the answer to their need for a kinsman redeemer himself.

'Don't go back to your mother-in-law empty handed' Ruth 3:17

Before he went up to the town gate where the city's business was conducted, he said to Ruth 'Bring me the shawl you are wearing and hold it out.' (Ruth 3:15). Then he poured into the shawl six measures of barley. The equivalent of this today is approximately 56 lbs or 25 kilograms of barley grain. That's quite a heavy load for a woman to carry, and it was an awful lot of food considering he was determined that their circumstances were now going to change. However, there may have been another reason for Boaz sending this large amount of grain home to her mother-in-law, than just supplying them with food. Boaz wasn't sure that he would be the one to marry Ruth, because there was a nearer relative that had the first option to do so. But, whether it was him or the nearer relative, this amount of grain could have supplied Naomi with a bridal dowry for Ruth to take into the marriage, in keeping with the marriage agreement that would be drawn up. We'll never know for sure but it may very well have been Boaz way of giving these impoverished women, not only a dowry but dignity, in the eyes of their community.

However, the best way to illustrate the value of the bridal dowry is to look at the parable that Jesus told in Luke's gospel, which is known as the parable of the lost coin.

'"Or what woman, having ten silver coins, if she loses one coin, does not light a lamp, sweep the house, and search carefully until she finds it? And when she has found it, she calls her friends and neighbours together, saying, 'Rejoice with me, for I have found the piece which I lost!' Likewise, I say to you, there is joy in the presence of the angels of God over one sinner who repents.'" Luke 15:8-10 (NKJV)

Without knowing the culture of that time we can't fully understand what Jesus was saying through this parable. To a modern day reader, there doesn't seem to be much similarity between the joy of finding a lost coin and the joy that is released in the presence of the angels when just one sinner repents. The joy of finding of a coin, even if it was silver seems quite meagre in comparison with a sinner finding salvation. Therefore, the depth of meaning in this parable is lost on us. But to all those standing around listening to Him the meaning would have been very clear.

They knew that when a bride was given money in the form of coins as a dowry to take into her marriage, she would sew those coins on to a headband that she would wear around her head. The dowry was her inheritance from her father, and it was to equip the bride for her new life with her husband. But the most important thing was that the dowry was her contribution to the marriage contract or covenant. Therefore if she lost one of those coins it would mean that she would not have the full and complete dowry. An incomplete dowry would be considered as a breach of the marriage contract; and that in turn would mean that she could not get married. So each and every coin making up that dowry was extremely important.

When she found the coin that she had lost she called together all her friends and neighbours to celebrate with her. The friends and neighbours would have been aware of the disaster that losing that coin would have been for her. Because there was no guarantee that her father would be able to find the money to make up the deficit. So the loss of that one coin could have affected her whole life and changed her future. That is why Jesus used this parable to compare and illustrate the joy of the angels when one sinner is saved.

Because finding the lost coin from her dowry was a momentous life changing occasion for the bride; and finding salvation, is an even more momentous life changing occasion for a lost sinner!

If Jesus our Bridegroom supplied His own blood as the bride price, as His contribution to the New Covenant contract, then what is our bridal dowry? What has been given to us by our Father to take into our new life with our husband as our inheritance?

I believe our heavenly Father has given us the most valuable dowry that we could ever receive. He has given us the 'Word of His grace'. His Word has given all of us who are sanctified and set apart for Jesus as His bride, a wonderful inheritance. Within the pages of scripture are to be found instruction and knowledge which are 'better than silver and gold' (Psalm 119:72) and wisdom that is 'more precious than rubies' (Proverbs 8:11).

When I looked up the phrase 'Word of His grace' in the original text, I found this literally means the Word of God 'breathed on' by His grace. This is a dowry that we are to wear, not on our head like the coins on the bride's headband in the parable, but *in* our head - and in our hearts too!

'Now I commit you to God and to the word of His grace, which can build you up and give you an *inheritance* among all those who are sanctified.' Acts 20:32

'Selah'

Chapter Six

Ceremonial Cleansing

The final stage in the Arrangement Period was the ceremonial cleansing. This came just before the beginning of the second stage of the wedding, which would begin with the Betrothal Ceremony.

Ceremonial cleansing was very important as a preparation for both the next stage of the wedding and for the Betrothal Ceremony itself. It symbolised the couple's spiritual cleansing; and it heralded the end of their old lives and the first step in their new lives as a betrothed couple, joined to each other through marriage.

The ceremony involved the bride and the groom separately, being immersed in water.

The Bride

'Repent and be baptised, every one of you, in the name of Jesus Christ for the forgiveness of your sins' Acts 2:38a

When we repent of our sins we are directed in Acts 2:38, and in other scriptures, to be baptised. The word translated as baptism is *baptizo* and it has the connotation of being submerged or overwhelmed; it is from the word that means to stain or to dye something. Baptism, being immersed in water is a declaration that our old life, which was subject to sin's directive, is at an end. It has been submerged and sunk.

'We were therefore buried with him through baptism into death in order that, just as Christ was raised from the dead through the glory of the Father, we too may live a new life.' Romans 6:4

The above scripture gives the best explanation and paints the clearest picture of what happens when we are baptised. It tells us that when we go under the water in baptism, it is symbolic of our old life being buried because it has died. Then, when we come up out of the water, we are symbolically being raised into a new life just as Christ was after His death. The act of baptism, in putting someone under the water and then bringing them up again, takes a matter of seconds. But those seconds are all it takes to make the declaration that our old life is dead and buried; it has been submerged and sunk; and we have been raised into a new life by the power of the Holy Spirit.

Also, in the picture language of the wedding, baptism represents our spiritual cleansing, making us ready and preparing us as the bride, who is to be joined to the Bridegroom for all eternity. In the light of this, it's not surprising that when I was baptised, and still in some places today, the one who is being baptised wears white!

The Groom

'The next day John saw Jesus coming towards him and said, "Look, the Lamb of God, who takes away the sin of the world!" John 1:29

Have you ever wondered why Jesus was baptised at the Jordan River; why He aligned Himself with all the people who had responded to John the Baptist's call to repent? If you have then you are not alone, because John the Baptist was surprised too.

'Then Jesus came from Galilee to the Jordan to be baptised by John. But John tried to deter him saying, "I need to be baptised by you, and do you come to me?" Jesus replied, "Let it be so now; it is proper for us to do this to fulfil all righteousness". Then John consented.' Matthew 3:13-15

We know through scripture that Jesus never gave in to temptation and therefore He didn't need to repent, or be cleansed from sin. So why did He ask John to baptise Him in water along with all those who responded to the call for repentance? In being baptised, Jesus was declaring that His old life was now dead, buried in the river Jordan; and the new life that had been planned and arranged for Him by His Father was just beginning. He was no longer Jesus the carpenter from Nazareth, son of Mary of Joseph's household. As He emerged from the Jordan River, He came out of the obscurity of His old life and into the limelight of His ministry as the Son of God, equipped for every good work. This new life, this new status, was immediately witnessed to and affirmed by His Father and the Holy Spirit.

'As soon as Jesus was baptised, he went up out of the water. At that moment heaven was opened, and he saw the Spirit of God descending like a dove and lighting on him. And a voice from heaven said, "This is my beloved Son, whom I love; with him I am well pleased."' Matthew 3:16-17

It was proper for Jesus 'to fulfil all righteousness' in making that declaration of dying to His old life and rising to the new life through baptism, even though only His Father and the Holy Spirit knew the full significance of it at the time. But it was also important for Jesus to comply with all that was required of Him as the Bridegroom in making Himself ready for the bride. By being baptised in water, He was undertaking the act of spiritual cleansing that heralded the beginning of the Betrothal Ceremony that was about to be embarked upon. It was the next step in the marriage that His Father had 'arranged' for Him, in which He would be joined to all those who were willing to accept Him as their groom; all those who were prepared to be spiritually cleansed too.

'Selah'

Chapter Seven

The Second Stage of the Wedding

The second stage of the wedding was the Betrothal period, which began with the Betrothal ceremony, called the *Kiddushin*, which comes from the Hebrew word that means 'sanctified' or 'set apart'. The *Kiddushin* reflects the sanctity of the ceremony about to be embarked upon; and it denotes that the couple are being set apart for a specific and sacred purpose, i.e. the marital relationship that is about to begin.

During the ceremony the couple are set apart for each other; but more specifically the woman was sanctified for the sacred purpose of being the bride of one particular man and no one else. This reflects the weddings we read about in Old Testament times when a man could have more than one wife, but a woman could only have one husband.

'May God himself, the God of peace, sanctify you through and through. May your whole spirit, soul, and body be kept blameless at the coming of our Lord Jesus Christ. The one who calls you is faithful and he will do it.' 1 Thessalonians 5:23-24

'For them I sanctify myself, that they too may be truly sanctified.' John 17:19

The Betrothal Ceremony

The Betrothal Ceremony took place under a *chuppah* or canopy in a public ceremony. It was under the *chuppah* that the bride and groom took their vows and declared the intent of their betrothal.

You may have been to a Jewish wedding; or seen films or pictures of a Jewish couple getting married, so you can probably picture what I'm saying. Because most modern Jewish weddings still take place under a *chuppah* or canopy today. The modern *chuppah* is usually a beautiful open-sided tent-like structure. The *chuppah* is said to be the symbol of the home that the new couple will build together. The reason for this 'home' having a roof without sides is that it represents the tent that the patriarch Abraham and his wife Sarah had. Their tent, it is said, was open on all sides to welcome people in unconditional hospitality.

The ceremony was and still is where possible, performed outside under an open sky, because of the promise that God gave to Abraham that his children shall be 'as numerous as the stars of heaven' (Genesis 15:5). Therefore, getting married outside under a *chuppah* is a desire for the married couple to have a hospitable home and be blessed with numerous children. How apt that is for us as His bride that we have this same desire - 'being given to hospitality' (Romans 12:13); and together with our Husband, be the means of reproducing many spiritual children!

In earlier days the *chuppah* wasn't an open sided, tent-like structure. It was the groom's prayer shawl or *tallit*, which he received as a young man at his bar-mitzvah. The bar-mitzvah being the ceremony that declares a Jewish male is no longer a boy, he is now a man. The prayer shawl would be held over the couple by four groomsmen each holding a pole that was attached to one of the corners of the shawl.

According to Wikipedia, the use of a *tallit* began in the Biblical period around 1800 BC. Therefore it is possible that Jesus, as a Jewish male would have been given a prayer shawl when He became a man. But whether He did have a prayer shawl or not, or if there was such a thing as a bar-mitzvah ceremony in those days, we don't know. But there is a clue in scripture as to when Jesus was no longer considered to be a boy, but a man. We find it in the only event recorded in scripture about Jesus' life between His birth and the beginning of His ministry.

'Every year his parents went to Jerusalem for the Feast of the Passover. When he was twelve years old, they went up to the Feast, according to the custom. After the Feast was over, while his parents were returning home, the boy Jesus stayed behind in Jerusalem, but they were unaware of it. Thinking he was in their company, they travelled on for a day. Then they began looking for him among their relatives and friends. When they did not find him, they went back to Jerusalem to look for him. After three days they found him in the temple courts, sitting among the teachers, listening to them and asking questions.

Everyone who heard him was amazed at his understanding and his answers. When his parents saw him, they were astonished. His mother said to him, "Son, why have you treated us like this? Your father and I have been anxiously searching for you." "Why were you searching for me?" he asked. "Didn't you know I had to be in my Father's house?" But they did not understand what he was saying to them.' Luke 2:41-52

In the above passage we read that when the Feast day was over, the twelve year old Jesus lingered behind in Jerusalem - but His parents didn't know it. So they had to return, another day's journey, back to Jerusalem to look for Him. If you have ever lost a child even for just a short while, you can imagine just how anxious they would have been on that return journey. Jesus had been missing for two days by the time they got back to Jerusalem; and then added to that we are told that it took them a further day before they eventually found Him sitting in the temple courts. They must have been astonished to find Him there listening to the teachers of the Law and asking them questions. But as loving parents, they couldn't understand how their Son could put them through such a nightmare scenario? It helps when reading this passage to know that the word used for Son here is *teknon*, which is not a word used for little children, it is a generic term for male offspring of any age in a family.

Have you ever asked yourself how Mary and Joseph could be so unaware of the fact that Jesus wasn't with them until the end of that first day on their journey home? For security reasons people tended to travel in groups. It kept them safe from the thieves and robbers that lay in wait for any unsuspecting traveller. We are told that Mary and Joseph asked among their friends and relatives if they had seen Him, which shows us that they probably thought He might be with another family during the day, maybe playing with their boys. But more recently, I found out there was a much more cultural reason for their not being aware that Jesus was missing on that journey home to Nazareth.

Apparently the women and children travelled together ahead of the men. At the end of the day they would set up a temporary campsite and get the evening meal ready. This meant that when the men arrived they would find the camp set up, and their meal 'on the table' ready for them to eat. So it's reasonable to suppose that Jesus travelled with His mother to Jerusalem with the women and children. Then when they arrived in Jerusalem the families joined the celebrations that marked the special and holy time called the Feast of Passover. We are told that Jesus was now twelve years old. It is around this age that a Jewish male is no longer considered to be a boy but a man. Visiting the temple during the Feast of Passover may very well have been the time when they officially marked this very important point in Jesus' life.

If this is correct, then Jesus wouldn't have been expected to set out on the return journey with the women and children. He would have been expected to travel back to Nazareth with the men and arrive at the camp after the women had set up the makeshift camp and prepared the evening meal. This would have made it very easy for Mary to think that Jesus was travelling behind with the men and her Joseph; and for Joseph to think that Jesus had mistakenly gone ahead of him with Mary, along with the other women and children, just as He had on the outward journey to Jerusalem - when He was still considered a boy. It would certainly explain why they only realised He was missing at the end of that day - when all the men arrived in camp and He wasn't with them.

This cultural explanation would also be a strong reason for Jesus to be in the temple courts with the teachers of the Law, listening to their discussions and asking questions. Because this wasn't something that women and children were allowed to do. The teachers of the Law must have considered Jesus to be a young man and no longer a boy, to have let Him be there with them. It would also explain why Jesus was perplexed that His parents didn't understand that He had to be about His heavenly Father's business - now that He was a man!

"My *prayer* is not for them alone. I *pray* also for those who will believe in me through their message."John 17:20

Whether Jesus was given a prayer shawl when He became a man, we will probably never know. But one thing we can be certain of is that Jesus' prayers drew us to Him and cover us now. We were included, when He prayed to His Father after that last meal He had with His disciples. 'I pray also for those who will believe' - this means us! We are one of 'those' who were reached through the message of salvation that was passed from disciple to disciple over the millennia of years that followed. His prayers helped us to be persuaded by the Holy Spirit to accept His offer to become His bride; and they covered us like a *chuppah*, as we took our vows of commitment to Him, declaring our intent to be 'set apart' unto Him. We came under the covering, under the protection of His *chuppah*, His prayer shawl then, and His prayers continue to cover, protect and direct us now.

'Therefore he is also able to save completely those who come to God through him, because he always lives to *intercede* for them.' Hebrews 7:25

Chapter Eight

The Cup

The inclusion of wine in any celebration is symbolic of joy in Jewish tradition. Wine is associated with Kiddush, the sanctification prayer recited on Shabbat. It plays a prominent part in all the Festivals; and of course wine was, and still is included in any Jewish wedding ceremony.

'He brought me to the banqueting house, and his banner over me was love.' (NKJV)

The word used for banqueting is the word *yayin*, which actually means wine, and as stated above, wine is symbolic of joy. Therefore being brought to the banqueting house is to be brought to a place of celebration and joy; brought into a joyful house where love is established as a banner over us.

In the Betrothal Ceremony, to see if his proposal was accepted, the young man poured a cup of wine for his bride, and then he waited to see if she drank it. Her acceptance of the cup of wine sealed and made legal the marriage contract, the marriage covenant.

In Old and New Testament times the shedding of blood was required to make covenants legal; but it wasn't appropriate to shed blood to seal a marriage covenant at weddings. Therefore, red wine was used as a symbolic substitute instead, probably because it is the same colour. Plus there are several references in scripture that link grapes, and the winepress with blood.

This practice of making a covenant by drinking from a cup has been passed on to us over the years in a way that we haven't always understood. You may have seen in films that depict olden times, where the conspirators come up with a plan and then lift up their drinking goblets and clink them together in agreement over their plan. Well that is a throwback to making a covenant. But this throwback has survived even to the present day. When someone says, "I'll drink to that" in agreement with someone else, whether holding a drink in their hand or not, you'll know that what they're saying comes from the practice of making a covenant and sealing it with wine, as a substitute for blood.

'Moses then took the blood, sprinkled it on the people and said, "This is the blood of the covenant that the LORD has made with you in accordance with all these words."' Exodus 24:8

Apart from weddings, blood was used in every other covenant between two or more people to seal them and make them legal. This was a practise that was accepted among all the nations surrounding Israel and beyond. Throughout Genesis we read that the LORD God made important covenants with Abraham, Isaac and Jacob, and all their descendants. They in turn made covenants with their neighbours to guarantee peace and harmony between themselves. These covenants were always confirmed by shedding the blood of animals, as seen in Genesis chapter 15 for example. However, when the Lord made the most important covenant He could with us - the New Covenant, it was He that supplied the blood to seal it and make it legal, not an animal. Our part is just to accept that His blood was shed for us; and confirm this by drinking from the cup in remembrance of Him, as He asked us to.

'Then he took *the cup*, gave thanks and offered it to them, and they all drank from it. "This is my blood of the covenant, which is poured out for many."' Mark 14:23-24

'In the same way, after supper he took *the cup*, saying, "This *cup* is the new covenant in my blood; do this in remembrance of me. For whenever you eat this bread and drink this *cup*, you proclaim the Lord's death until he comes."' 1 Corinthians 11:25-26

As we drink from 'the cup' in remembrance of Jesus, whether we call it Communion, the Eucharist, or the Lord's

Supper we are confirming our acceptance of the New Covenant that was sealed and made legal by the shedding of His precious blood at the cross. Plus we are confirming our acceptance of Him as our Bridegroom, and sealing the marriage covenant we have with our heavenly Husband.

NB: There are beneficial compounds in wine which include antioxidants; but there is also a chemical called resveratrol, which among other things has been shown to have a cardio protective effect. In other words this chemical is good for the heart. The chemical is produced naturally by the grape skins when they are exposed to yeast during fermentation. This means that resveratrol is found mainly in red wine because white wine has minimal contact with the grape skins during the fermentation process, and generally contains lower levels of this chemical.

However, most of the resveratrol doesn't reach the blood circulation when drinking wine in the normal way. To benefit fully from the resveratrol in red wine, it is recommended that it is sipped slowly. That way it is absorbed into the blood via the mucous membranes in the mouth. Apparently, sipping the wine is said to be one hundred times more beneficial than just drinking it straight down!

Therefore, when you take a sip from 'the cup' containing red wine, in remembrance of Him, take your time to savour exactly what Jesus has done for you. Because as you do, you are not only remembering that His blood has been shed for you - you are also improving your own blood. You are absorbing resveratrol and thus protecting your heart and improving the blood circulation throughout the whole of your body. Isn't this just amazing! And so is our Saviour — He's amazing!

'Selah'

Chapter Nine

The Ring

Something of value was given to the bride and it had to be the groom's own property. He couldn't borrow it from a friend or a relative, but it could be given to him by someone else as a gift. It wasn't a case of 'purchasing' a wife, as she wasn't to be considered in terms of being owned like a piece of property or a slave. The bride's acceptance of the valuable item was, like the cup, also considered as her acceptance of the groom, and the contract he offered. The item of value that the Groom gave would have been written into the contract from the beginning and was usually a ring. It's no coincidence that a ring has been incorporated as a legal requirement in our modern marriages today.

In days gone by a ring could be used as a seal. All seals, including those set into rings, were personal to their owners and enabled other people to recognise who they belonged to. In the case of letters, documents and scrolls a seal was used to identify who the writer or sender was. They would light a candle and let the wax drip onto the paper or parchment. Then they would press their seal into the soft wax. As letters and documents were sent and delivered by hand, the sender would fold or roll up his document and seal the folded edge using the wax. This made the letter, document or scroll safe, because it couldn't be surreptitiously opened by another person before it reached its legitimate destination, without their having to break the waxed seal and thus give themselves away.

Seals were also used for things other than documents to make them safe from deception or robbery. For instance, when Jesus was taken down from the cross the chief priests and Pharisees went to Pilate and insisted that His tomb was made secure. They remembered that Jesus had said that He would rise from the dead after three days. They didn't believe it, but they were worried that His disciples would try to steal His body away and then say that He had risen. So Pilate told them, "Take a guard and go make the tomb as secure as you know how." So they went and made the tomb secure by putting a seal on the stone and posting a guard.' (Matthew 27:65-66). We're not told if the seal was broken or if it remained intact when the stone was rolled away - but such things weren't a problem for the angel who rolled the stone back and then sat on it!

In all matters a seal made an impression that was as effective as someone's signature is today. It made documents legal and it was a guarantee that something was genuine. A seal's validation meant, and still means, that a legal document or a governmental decree cannot be revoked or reversed. For example if someone makes a will only another will made by the same person can override the original.

This can be clearly seen in the story of Esther. When her uncle Mordecai tells Esther of Haman's plot to destroy the Jews, she risks her life in agreeing to speak to her husband the king about it. After paying him the compliment of inviting him to two delicious banquets she tells him of the evil plot, which means not only the death of all the Jews in his provinces but her death too, as she was also a Jew. The king is horrified but he tells her the decree that he signed, which validated Haman's plot could not be changed, altered or made invalid. The only way to deal with this situation, the only way she could overrule and change what had already been written, sealed, and sent out to the king's provinces beforehand, was to write another decree.

"Now write another decree in the king's name on behalf of the Jews as seems best to you, and *seal* it with the king's signet ring - for no document written in the king's name and *sealed* with his ring can be revoked." Esther 8:8

The King of kings has sent out a decree. It is known as the New Covenant. It has been, and still is being sent out to all the King's provinces, to all the territories that are under His rule by His emissaries, His disciples. However, we can rest assured that there will never be another legal document issued that will overrule, change, or revoke that. This decree, this covenant was written and sealed in the King's name by the Holy Spirit; and our King Himself has paid a high price to make it legal.

'In Him you also trusted, after you heard the word of truth, the gospel of your salvation; in whom also, having believed, you were *sealed* with the Holy Spirit of promise, who is the guarantee of our inheritance...' Ephesians 1:13-14 (NKJV)

When you gave your life to Christ, when you were 'born again', you were 'sealed' with the Holy Spirit. He has pressed His seal into your life as a guarantee that you are His and that you have an inheritance. To put this in another way, the Lord our God has put His signature upon you!

'... He anointed us, set his *seal* of ownership on us, and put his Spirit in our hearts as a deposit, guaranteeing what is to come.' 2 Corinthians 1:22-23

As we live our daily lives, often unknown to us, we are displaying the fact that we are His, that we have His signature, His seal imprinted upon us. I remember as a non-Christian looking at believers and thinking, "There is something different about them", but I couldn't say what it was. Now I know it was because they had His seal upon them, the seal of the Holy Spirit. The Holy Spirit witnesses to the world, through us that God is genuine. At the same time He witnesses to us, that our eternal inheritance is genuine too. In fact He guarantees it!

'You, yourselves are our letter, written on our hearts, known and read by everybody. You show that you are a letter from Christ, the result of our ministry, written not with ink but with the Spirit of the living God, not on tablets of stone but on tablets of human hearts.' 2 Corinthians 3:2-3

We have been given the Ring, the Seal of the Holy Spirit as a guarantee that our marriage contract with the King of all kings will never be revoked, terminated or overturned.

Chapter Ten

The Blessing

A vital part of any Jewish wedding, both then and now are the blessings. In modern Jewish weddings the *Kiddushin* and *Nissuin* are combined into one service, and they include seven blessings, which are given by the Rabbi, members of the family and selected guests. These blessings include prayers and they acknowledge that marriage is God-given and central to life.

How different this is in a world where couples can now choose to have their wedding in any number of venues here or abroad. Where they are able to plan and arrange their wedding around the main focus of a particular theme, the location they have flown to, or around the venue itself. It's sad to think that all these things can make up the central theme of weddings today and the Lord isn't even thought of, let alone blessed and honoured.

We don't have any firm understanding as to how many blessings were given in biblical times, but there is no doubt that blessing would have played an important part of their wedding ceremonies. That is because blessing was very important and taken very seriously, as was cursing.

Blessing was so important to Jacob that he cheated and deceived his father in order to get the blessing due to his twin brother. Esau was the eldest by only a matter of minutes, but never the less he was the one designated to receive their father's blessing (see Genesis 27). However, Jacob didn't fair too well from cheating to get that blessing. It meant he had to leave his home and family and work for another just like himself, his cheating uncle and father-in-law Laban. He worked hard for this man until such time as he left and made his peace with his brother Esau.

Throughout the book of Genesis we read that God made incredible promises to Abraham, Isaac and Jacob; and all those promises were accompanied with His blessings. From these three men the nation of Israel was formed, through natural multiplication during the 400 years they spent in the land of Egypt. Whereas God had previously blessed individuals directly, once they became a nation He decided to bless them through His representatives on earth, who were the priesthood. Aaron and his sons were the first to be given this honour; but it was a perpetual commandment that was to continue on down through the priestly line in the centuries that would follow. Blessing the people in this way didn't preclude God's ability to bless anyone personally, but it did show His intent that all His people should receive and benefit from His blessing.

'The LORD said to Moses, "Tell Aaron and his sons, 'This is how you are to *bless* the Israelites. Say to them: The LORD bless you and keep you; the LORD make his face shine on you and be gracious to you; the LORD turn his face towards you and give you peace. So they will put my name on the Israelites, and I will bless them.'"' Numbers 6:22-27

How privileged we are that through the New Covenant we, as His people are able to receive His blessing personally and not just corporately. Jesus, our High Priest has blessed us beyond imagination. Through His sacrifice He has removed the barrier that prevented our coming close to Him; and He has sent the Holy Spirit to impart to us every blessing there is in heavenly places.

'Praise be to the God and Father of our Lord Jesus Christ, who has *blessed us* in the heavenly realms with every spiritual blessing in Christ.' Ephesians 1:3

To bless someone is to do more than wish nice things for them. Blessing is linked to honouring them. In Genesis 49 we read that Jacob, on his deathbed, called his twelve sons together to tell them what would happen to them in the future and to bestow his blessings upon them. But because his three eldest sons had acted wickedly against him or their neighbours, they forfeited the blessing of the eldest son. So this special blessing was given to Judah who was next in line. It's worth noting here that both David and Jesus were descended from the tribe of Judah. They were in the line that had inherited the blessing of the eldest son. It had been passed on down through the centuries beginning with and directly from, the patriarchs, Abraham, Isaac and Jacob.

On his deathbed, Jacob addressed each son in turn and in refusing to bless those three elder sons he said, 'Let not my honour be united with them.' (Genesis 49:6 - NKJV). The word for honour is the same word that is used for glory in other places in scripture. This makes it clear that to bless someone is to impart some of your honour to them, to bestow some of your glory on them, as well as asking God to be favourable towards them. As believers, we too have inherited the blessing of the eldest son, not because of what we have done or not done, but because scripture tells us we have been made co-heirs with Christ. Therefore, being the recipients of His blessing, we are also the recipients of His honour; and His glory too. Now that's something really worth remembering when life tells us differently!

'The Spirit himself testifies with our spirit that we are God's children. Now if we are children, then we are heirs - heirs of God and co-heirs with Christ.' Romans 8:16-17a

Having been blessed and given honour from God ourselves, we have the ability to pass on and impart that blessing to others. But more importantly we should return it back to Him - in praise and thanksgiving; and in honouring and glorifying His name.

'Praise, O servants of the LORD, praise the name of the LORD. Let the name of the LORD be praised both now and for evermore.' Psalm 113:1-2

'To him who sits on the throne and to the Lamb be praise and honour and glory and power for ever and ever!' Revelation 5:13b

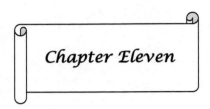

Chapter Eleven

After the Ceremony

After the ceremony, when the second stage of the wedding was completed, the bride and groom didn't go off on honeymoon; and they didn't go to their own home to live together as man and wife. Even though they had made their vows committing themselves to each other, they were not allowed to live together as man and wife for a period of about a year. Instead they returned to their own homes and resumed their normal lives, with their own families - their parents and their siblings. But at this stage, even though they had not, and would not sleep together, their vows were taken so seriously and were so binding that it would need a divorce to separate them.

The reason they had to wait for approximately a year before they lived and slept together was to establish proof of the bride's purity. It was to make sure, without any doubt that she was not pregnant by another man when she took her vows. The usual gestation period for carrying a child in pregnancy is nine months. But without the benefit of pregnancy tests and ultrasound scans the due date was always subject to a certain amount of inaccuracy. So in order to make sure the bride wasn't pregnant, they had to allow a substantial leeway for getting the dates wrong. They decided that a margin of three months would achieve that, and so it was accepted that approximately a year should pass between the second and third stages of the wedding. That way they made certain that the bride was not carrying another man's child prior to the groom's completing his marriage commitment to her; before he brought her into his bed, and brought her into his family.

When the Nation of Israel took possession of the land promised to them by the LORD God all those centuries before, it was divided up by Joshua between the tribes. Then the individual tribes allocated a piece of their allotted land to the individual families that made up their tribe. Land wasn't just something to live on and work on. Land established who they were in the history and genealogy of their tribes and in their nation.

This made waiting for a year after the betrothal ceremony very, very important, because the family's land was tied up with a man's inheritance; and they had to make sure that 'their' land stayed with 'their' family. If the bride had slept with another man and was expecting his baby, then that child, if it turned out to be a boy, could inherit the land that had been in the groom's family for generations. It was impossible to think of another family's child, or even worse the child of another tribe, inheriting 'their' land and corrupting the seamless thread of inheritance that had been passed on to them by their forefathers.

It's when we understand this that we can understand why the sin of adultery was punished, in a way that we can't comprehend in today's modern way of thinking - by stoning to death. I doubt if they had much in the way of contraception other than abstinence. Therefore, committing adultery wasn't just the betrayal of their wedding vows and the pain of broken relationships. Adultery meant there was the potential to defraud families of their land, their lineage and their God-given inheritance by means of an illegitimate heir being born into their family.

It was probably why the religious leaders, spoken of in John chapter eight, decided they only needed to stone the woman who was caught in adultery and not the man, even though the law said to stone both. Men weren't likely to have a child as a result of their actions whereas women were. So I guess that was at least part of the reason for their prejudice in bringing only the woman before Jesus, even though the man must have been there when she was taken; because we are told that they caught the woman in the 'act' of adultery (see John 8:1-11).

'Now the birth of Jesus Christ was as follows: After His mother Mary was betrothed to Joseph, before they came together, she was found with child of the Holy Spirit. Then Joseph her husband, being a just man, and not wanting to make her a public example, was minded to put her away secretly.' Matthew 1:18-19 (NKJV)

When Mary conceived Jesus by the Holy Spirit, she wasn't engaged to Joseph and she wasn't married to him in the full sense of the word, because she was a virgin. The situation was that Mary and Joseph had been through the Betrothal Ceremony as above. They had completed the first two stages of the wedding but the third and final stage was yet to come; and only after that last stage would they be able to consummate their marriage. Mary was God's choice to conceive His Son by the Holy Spirit, but He was aware that she needed a husband to take care of her, and His Son. So He chose this important time, between the vows of betrothal and the final vows that were to be taken later on, to send the angel with the good news.

The word used in Matthew that describes Joseph as being 'a just man', can also be translated as 'a righteous man'. In checking out the concordance, I found that the word also means that Joseph was 'approved and acceptable' to God. So the Lord's choice of Mary, as the woman to bring His Son to birth, also included the fact that she was betrothed to Joseph – a righteous, acceptable man of whom He approved.

When Mary told him she was pregnant, I wonder if Joseph had assumed that she had broken her vows and been unfaithful to him. Or did he think that she had been compromised by another man against her will? If so that would mean that she wouldn't be stoned, but she would be obliged to marry the father of her child according to the law (see Deuteronomy 22:23-29). Well we'll never know what he had been thinking. But being a betrothed couple, and having taken vows that were strong and binding, Joseph would have had to initiate a divorce to separate them. But being a righteous man, he didn't want to expose her to public humiliation and / or any possibility of being stoned. So we are told in Matthew's gospel that 'he had in mind to divorce her quietly' Matthew 1:19.

Thank goodness the angel of the Lord appeared to him in a dream and gave him the good news about Mary's condition. However I'm guessing that in not divorcing her, their families, friends, and the community would have surmised that Joseph was the cause of Mary's pregnancy rather than the unlikely explanation of it being due to the Holy Spirit! This reaction would have been very unpleasant for the couple, but having taken their betrothal vows they were able to proceed towards the third and final stage of their wedding.

Chapter Twelve

The Gifts

When the Betrothal ceremony, the *Kiddushin* was over, before he left and went to his family home, the groom would give his bride gifts. The gifts were to remind her, during the time they were apart, that he was thinking of her and that he would return for her when the time came for the final ceremony.

Gifts were always involved in celebrations and offerings to the LORD God, or to any idols. Plus they were very useful for appeasing an enemy, showing friendship or giving as a bribe. Fathers gave gifts to their children and now we see that the groom gave gifts to his bride. But we have been given the greatest gift of all.

'When He ascended on high, he led captives in his train and gave *gifts* to men' Ephesians 4:8

'Repent and be baptised, every one of you, in the name of Jesus Christ for the forgiveness of sins. And you will receive *the gift* of the Holy Spirit.' Acts 2:38

Included with *the gift* of the Holy Spirit are spiritual gifts, which are described in 1 Corinthians 12. 'All these are the work of one and the same Spirit, and He gives them to each one, just as He determines.' (v.11) 'They are given to us to use in works of power, on His behalf, for 'the common good' (v.7) But there are also other more 'personal' gifts that our Bridegroom has left us to remember Him by....

'.... the *gift* of righteousness' Romans 5:17b

To be given the gift of righteousness is to be given something amazing. A good definition of righteousness is, 'to be as we ought to be - acceptable to God'. We are given this gift as a consequence of faith. Romans 4:3-4 tells us that faith has been 'credited' to us as righteousness. In terms that we can understand these days, we could say that faith has paid off our credit card debt and given us a brand new debit card of righteousness. Or to put it another way, it's like someone paying off all our outstanding debts and then putting money into our bank account for us to draw on!

The gift of righteousness means that we are able to stand in Father's Presence without a sense of fear, condemnation or inferiority. It means that we can boldly approach the 'throne of grace' (Hebrews 4:16) and ask for what we need. It's like going to the bank manager, knowing that all our debts have been paid and that we have a very healthy bank balance. There is no fear of our being rejected through lack of funds, which means we are able ask with confidence!

At the cross, Jesus paid off all our debts with His life and He earned enough righteousness to provide healthy debit cards of righteousness to all those who believe in Him and commit their lives to Him.

There is no way that we could have paid our sin debt with our own righteousness. Scripture tells us quite clearly that our righteousness is like 'filthy rags' (Isaiah 64:6). In fact, our righteousness is a bit like the now defunct French franc or the German mark. Our righteousness is like old currency from another nation. It's not valid in God's kingdom! So Jesus gave us righteousness as a gift, which is kingdom currency that is validated by the bank of heaven.

'... *the gift* of God is eternal life in Christ Jesus our Lord.' Romans 6:23b

Another gift we have been given is the gift of eternal life. But eternal life isn't something for the future. Eternal life is ours now. It's a present day and continuous reality. It began when we were 'born again, by the Spirit of God' (see John 3:6-8). The phrase 'born again' is easier to understand when we know that it is better translated as 'born from above' by the Spirit of God. Our natural life began when we were born by our earthly mother; but when we accepted Jesus as our Saviour, although we still looked the same, our spirits were born from above. That new birth was the beginning of our spiritual life as children of our Heavenly Father. It's a life that is eternal, it continues beyond this physical life and into the next.

'I became a servant of this gospel by the *gift* of God's grace...' Ephesians 3:7a

'For it is by grace you have been saved through faith - and this not from yourselves, it is the *gift* of God' Ephesians 2:8

This gift of grace equips us and facilitates all that He has called us to be and to do. I recently found a definition of grace that I believe helps us to understand what grace is and how it operates – 'Grace is the merciful kindness which God uses to bring about holy influence upon souls in turning them to Christ. It keeps, strengthens and increases them in Christian faith, knowledge and affection; and it spurs them on to be active in pursuing Christian qualities.'

The word grace has been translated from the Greek word *charis*. This word can also be translated as good will, loving-kindness and favour. Therefore, we have not only been given the gift of God's grace, we have been given so much more including the gift of God's favour. I looked up the word favour in an ordinary, non biblical dictionary and found this definition - liking, approval; a kindly or helpful act beyond what is due; favouritism; a badge or ornament worn to show that one supports a certain party.

This last bit reminded me of the time when knights of old would go forth on their trusty steeds to do battle in a jousting contest. According to the films I've seen of that era, before the contest began the knights would bow before the king on his throne. The king would be surrounded by the nobility who were there to watch the contest. When the formalities were over a noble lady would give the knight of her choice her token or her 'favour' to wear. The token or 'favour' showed that she was supporting him in the ensuing contest against his rival. It was to bring him good fortune and keep him safe in the battle.

The One who loves and supports us has given us the gift of His 'favour', to bless us and keep us safe in the battles that we face in this world, until the time that all such battles are over and we are safe in His arms.

'Therefore you do not lack any spiritual *gift* as you eagerly wait for our Lord Jesus Christ to be revealed.' 1 Corinthians 1:7

When He left this earth, our Bridegroom gave us gifts to remember Him by and to demonstrate that He is thinking about us while we are apart. He gave us the gift of His Holy Spirit, who in turn gives us the gifts of ministry and power for the 'common good' when we need them. Plus He gave us personal gifts, including the gift of His righteousness that we can bank on; His gift of eternal life, which begins at salvation; and the gifts of His grace and His favour to help us on a daily basis. All these gifts were given to us, not because of what we have done or who we are. His generosity is based on the fact that we have accepted Who He is, and what He has done. We could not earn these wonderful, incredible gifts in a million years; and it's so encouraging to know that once they have been given to us, scripture says that they won't ever be taken away or made invalid!

'For God's *gifts* and his call are irrevocable' Romans 11:29

'Selah'

Chapter Thirteen

The Groom's Preparation

Before the groom returned to his home after the betrothal ceremony, he would encourage his bride by telling her that he would be preparing the place they would share together as man and wife, while they were apart. When it was ready he would come for her and the final stage of their wedding would take place.

In those days young married couples didn't have their own homes; the place he would get ready for them to live in would be a room in, or added onto his father's house. During the year he and his bride were apart it was the groom's job to spend all his spare time in getting that place ready.

"In My Father's house are many *rooms*; if it were not so, I would have told you. I am going there to *prepare a place* for you. And if I go and *prepare a place* for you, I will *come back* and take you to be with me that you also may be where I am." John 14:2-3

Jesus wanted to reassure His disciples that He wouldn't leave them forever that He would definitely return for them. So He used the 'well known' illustration of the groom preparing a place in his father's house before claiming his bride and taking her to be with him there. The disciples would have understood this as it was a custom of their day.

'I am the vine; you are the branches. If a man remains in me and I in Him, he will bear much fruit; apart from me you can do nothing.' John 15:5

Some bible translations use the words 'In My Father's house are many mansions' instead of 'many rooms', but in the light of the Jewish wedding I think the word rooms is probably more appropriate. The word translated as room or mansion means - staying, abiding, dwelling, to make ones abode. One day we will stay or abide with Him in the heavenly place that He has prepared for us in His Father's house. But in the meantime He calls us to remain or abide with Him while living here on earth - so that we can bear much fruit.

However there are many things that come at us in life that unsettle us and we find it difficult to rest in Him and be at peace. So how do we stay in a place of abiding?

I have always thought that the words 'staying level' make the concept of abiding a bit easier to understand. For example, when people are annoyed with us, or being downright difficult, we can't necessarily change how they feel or how they are reacting. But it is possible to take control of what is happening to us. If we can stay level and keep our own peace, then we can watch them going up or down on their emotional see-saw and not be affected by it ourselves. It takes practice to stay level, but the more we do it, the better we will get. Abiding will free us up to be who we are and allow our spirit, rather than our emotions to lead us in fruitful ways.

'No one knows about that day or hour, not even the angels in heaven, nor the Son, but *only the Father*.' Matthew 24:36

The bridegroom's preparation of the room was very important and he wasn't allowed to skimp on the work. He had to make sure he made a really good job of it. The reason being, that he couldn't move on to the final stage of the wedding, and consummate his marriage, until the room was considered ready and fit for purpose by his father. It was then and only then, when he had his father's approval that he was allowed to go and claim his bride. So if anyone asked him when the final stage of his wedding would take place, he would reply, "Only my father knows!"

Using the analogy of the groom returning for his bride was Jesus' way of telling His disciples that He didn't know the timing of His own return. It wasn't up to Him; it was up to His Father. The picture language of the wedding was the easiest and clearest way to explain that to them. But because this was so culturally relevant, like many other pictures and parables that Jesus spoke, the full understanding of what He was trying to convey has been lost to most of us over the years since then. But now we know for sure that He is definitely coming back for us. But that will be only when His Father says so - *"Only My Father knows!"*

'Selah'

Chapter Fourteen

The Bride's Preparation

In the meantime, while the groom was preparing their room, the bride would go home to her father's house. As she waited for the day when they would complete their wedding vows she would prepare beautiful wedding garments to wear at the final stage of the wedding. While he put his energy into preparing a place for them to live together, she put all her thoughts and preparations into making herself ready for him and their new life together, by making herself as pure and beautiful as she could be.

When Esther was picked out as a potential bride for King Xerxes she and all the other potential brides, were taken to his harem under the care of Hegai, the king's trusted eunuch. There they were given a twelve month beauty treatment, 'six months with oil of myrrh and six months with perfumes and cosmetics' (see Esther 2:12). The girls were pampered and massaged with the best beauty products available. When it was their turn to go to the king, their skin must have been smooth as silk and they must have smelt absolutely wonderful!

'.... what kind of people ought you to be? You ought to live holy and godly lives as you look forward to the day of God and speed its coming..... make every effort to be found spotless, blameless and at peace with him.' 2 Peter 3:11 & 14b

We have a King who desires to spend time with us, not just for one night as happened for most of those girls from the harem, but frequently. He wants us, like Esther to be there as His bride at His side at any time of the day or night.

But what do we need to do to make ourselves ready for our Bridegroom? What needs to be massaged into our life to make us smell heavenly and irresistible to Him? What gives us access into His presence at any time day or night? Worship! Worship in spirit and truth not only rises up to Him as a sweet fragrant aroma, but it also affects the quality and sweetness of our lives too. It is by entering His presence with praise, love and thanksgiving; and by keeping ourselves special for Him and not letting the smell of foolishness and unconfessed sin spoil the precious ointment (see Ecclesiastes 10:1). That is how we can be as pure and beautiful as we can be, as we wait for our Bridegroom to come.

'But just as he who called you is holy, so be holy in all you do' 1 Peter 1:15

In biblical times the high priest wasn't able to minister to the LORD God in the holy places unless he wore holy garments. According to the above scriptures the pure, beautiful garment we are to wear is holiness, which is not an outward piece of clothing but an inward way of life. But holiness seems quite a daunting word in itself, let alone trying to achieve it. But let me encourage you, holiness isn't something beyond our reach.

The word 'holy' is the Greek word *hagios,* which can also be translated as 'saint'. "Oh no!" you might say, "I could never be a saint!" But you already are! If you have been born again, born from above, then you are no longer classed as a sinner, one who habitually sins, you are now classed as a saint. When ending his letter to the Philippians, Paul sends his greetings to all the saints in Christ Jesus; and goes on to say that all the saints in Philippi send their greetings to them (see Philippians 4:21-22). The scriptural description of being a saint isn't a special title for those who have achieved spiritual greatness; it is just another name for all those who believe in Him. All those who are children born of the Holy Spirit, the *Hagios Pneuma.*

As His bride, all we need to do in order to make sure our garments are pure and beautiful, is to ask for forgiveness whenever we mess up; and to give forgiveness to those who

'At that time the kingdom of heaven will be like ten virgins who took their lamps and went out to meet the bridegroom. Five of them were foolish and five of them were wise. The foolish ones took their lamps but did not take any oil with them. The wise however, took oil in jars along with their lamps. The bridegroom was a long time coming and they all became drowsy and fell asleep.

At midnight the cry rang out: 'Here's the bridegroom! Come out to meet him!'

Then all the virgins woke up and trimmed their lamps. The foolish ones said to the wise, 'Give us some of your oil; our lamps are going out.'

'No,' they replied, 'there may not be enough for both us and you. Instead, go to those who sell oil and buy some for yourselves.'

But while they were on their way to buy the oil, the bridegroom arrived. The virgins who were ready went in with him to the wedding banquet. And the door was shut.

Later the others also came, 'Sir! Sir!' they said, 'Open the door for us!'

But he replied, 'I tell you the truth, I don't know you.'

Therefore keep watch, because you do not know the day or the hour.' Matthew 25:1-13

This parable came about as a result of the disciples asking Jesus to tell them about the 'end of the age'. They wanted to know when it would take place and what would be the sign of His coming back to earth for the second and final time (see Matthew 24:3). This questioning came when they were in Jerusalem for what would be their last week together, before Jesus was arrested and crucified. Jesus had already shared a lot of important things with His disciples during those last days because He knew that it was His last opportunity to tell them what they needed to know.

In Matthew 25, having told them about the physical signs that would herald the coming of the end times, Jesus continues by telling them what they personally needed to know in order to be prepared for the 'end of the age' and His return. He wasn't able to tell them the exact time frame of when this would happen, so He used the illustration of the bride and her virgin companions waiting for the bridegroom to come. This was a perfect way for Him to warn them to be ready, alert and watchful. They would have attended many weddings and I'm sure their mother and sisters would have told them all that was involved in this stage of the proceedings.

'Behold, I come like a thief! Blessed is he who stays awake and keeps his clothes with him, so that he may not go naked and be shamefully exposed.' Revelation 16:15

There were ten virgins and the number ten in Jewish circles denotes the number of ordinal perfection required for any spiritual assembly; and the fact that they were virgins and not married women speaks of purity. Over the years many eminent theologians have given their thoughts on the significance of the virgins, their lamps and the oil; as well as acknowledging that being watchful and alert is the message of this parable. However I would like to look at it in a different way.

The virgins were with the bride as her companions, as she waited for the groom to come; and the groom had his companions or groomsmen with him when he arrived. In the next chapter you will see that the companions of our Groom will be the angels. This made me ask the question, 'Who or what are the pure, virginal companions that are with us as the bride here on earth as we wait for Him to come?' Into my mind came the scripture, 'Your word is a lamp unto my feet and a light unto my path' Psalm 119:105.

The Word of God written under the inspiration of the Holy Spirit is a pure, virgin companion to all believers. It has illuminated the ways and character of God to a fallen world over thousands of years. But the Word can be 'dry' sometimes. It can be just like a lamp without oil. It can, and often has been taught in a dry and legalistic way, instead of bringing life and light to those being instructed. Throughout the ages man's interpretation of the Word of God has sadly been the cause of arguments, which have led to 'foolish' decisions being taken by those who profess to be His. Many of these arguments have led to doctrinal differences that have divided the church again and again.

So may I suggest, for the purposes of this book at least, that the lamp of the Word without the ongoing illuminating oil of the Holy Spirit represents the five foolish virgins? Virgins who, having begun with a measure of oil (Spirit inspired writing), have ended up with the legalistic foolishness of the flesh - 'Are you so foolish? Having begun in the Spirit, are you now being made perfect by the flesh?' (Galatians 3:3). Using the same analogy, the five wise virgins would represent the pure virginal lamp of the Word, which continues to be illuminated by the oil of the Holy Spirit and His inspired revelation.

All the virgins should have had a small container of oil to accompany their lamps, so that when their lamps went out they could refill them. As the waiting, betrothed bride, we need to have as our virgin companions, the lamp of the Word and the oil of the Spirit. We need them both to make us ready to greet our Groom when Jesus returns in the end times. But if we are foolish enough to neglect the need for such a precious commodity as the illuminating oil of the Spirit before that time, there will be no time to seek it out at the end of the age.

NB: Oil was and is used for more than just for the purposes of light. It was used for man's health and welfare in a multitude of ways. But oil is only released when olives are crushed, either in a mortar or in an olive press. Our Lord Jesus Christ, as with the olives, willingly allowed Himself to be crushed - for our health and welfare in a multitude of ways. It began in the olive grove of Gethsemane. He prayed with such anguish that it caused His emotions to be crushed to the extent that it squeezed the blood out through the pores of His skin along with the perspiration (see Luke 22:44). Then He was arrested and crushed by the brutality of the Roman soldiers, who took Him and flogged Him within an inch of His life. Then they mocked Him and struck Him on the head, upon which they had rammed a crown of vicious thorns (see Mark 15:15-20).

The crushing continued as He struggled to get air into His lungs while hanging on that cross in Golgotha; and finally He experienced the most crushing thing of all. For the very first time in His life He knew separation from His Father. He had been with His Father from the beginning, before time began; and when He came to earth He was in constant communion with Him. But on the cross as sin engulfed all of Jesus in every way, His Father had to turn away. He could not look on sin, so He could not look upon His Son. The rejection Jesus felt when His Father turned away from Him crushed His Spirit in such a way that we could never imagine. But He was willing to experience that crushing rejection from His Father because His rejection meant our acceptance.

Without Jesus being so consummately crushed in every way, the oil of the Holy Spirit could not have been released and poured out on such an undeserving, but truly loved world!

'Selah'

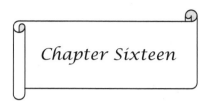

Chapter Sixteen

The Return of the Bridegroom

When the groom's father was happy that everything was as it should be, he would tell his son, *"All is ready; now is the time. You may go and claim your bride."* That would be the signal for the groomsmen to set out ahead of the groom and the wedding party, towards the bride's home.

Leading the procession, the groomsmen would shout out informing everyone that the bridegroom was coming. This would be followed by a loud blast on the *shofar* horn, which was their equivalent of our trumpet. The sound of the *shofar* told everybody that the bridegroom was on his way.

'At midnight the cry rang out: *"Here is the bridegroom! Come out to meet him!"* Matthew 25:6

'For the Lord Himself will come down from heaven, with a *loud command*, with the *voice* of the archangel and with the *trumpet call* of God...' 1Thessalonians 4:16

When the bride and her virgin companions heard the shouting of the groomsmen and the blast on the *shofar* horn they would go out to meet the groom, with their lamps alight as he came to claim his bride. Then the whole wedding party, those who had come with the groom, those who had been waiting at the bride's house, plus all those who had come out to meet the bridegroom, returned to the groom's house for the final stage of the wedding.

'We believe that Jesus died and rose again and so we believe that God will *bring with Jesus* those who have fallen asleep in him...... After that, we who are still alive and are left will be caught up *together with them* in the clouds to meet the Lord in the air. And so we will be with the Lord forever.' 1Thessalonians 4:14 & 17

'But the day of the Lord will come like a thief. The heavens will disappear with a roar; the elements will be destroyed by fire, and the earth and everything in it will be laid bare.' 2 Peter 3:10

In those days, without the benefit of electricity, or even gas to light their streets, people didn't usually leave their homes at night. Night, according to the concordance, apart from being the time when work ceased and people slept, was the time for deeds of sin and shame; and the time of moral stupidity. In other words the people who did go out at night were usually up to no good. Thieves and robbers especially took advantage of night time to carry out their dark deeds.

It was because thieves and robbers were out and about at night time under the cover of darkness, that the people made a joke of saying that the bridegroom was coming like a thief to 'steal' his bride. Well it certainly was his intent to take her away from her home and family and take her back with him!

'They will see the Son of Man coming on the clouds of the sky, with power and great glory. And he will send his angels with a loud trumpet call and they will gather his elect from the four winds, from one end of heavens to the other.' Mathew 24:3-31

Can you imagine the sight! Angels who heralded His first coming, filling the sky, announcing His arrival on earth - for the second time. Announcing that He is coming, not as a baby this time, but as He is now our glorious, glorified risen Lord! The Bridegroom of our hearts desire, returning to earth, to the place He left for the bride He is betrothed to; coming for all who have waited and longed for His appearing. He's coming back for you and me!

'The Lord is not slow in keeping his promise, as some understand slowness. He is patient with you, not wanting anyone to perish, but everyone to come to repentance... You ought to live holy and godly lives as you look forward to the day of God and speed its coming' 2 Peter 3:9 & 11-12a

Therefore let us be ready. Not letting our love grow cold or allowing our lamps to grow dim by neglecting His Word and the guidance of the Holy Spirit. As we wait for His return, let us be diligent in serving Him and in reaching out to the lost, so that the number of those who are known as His bride is increased. Let us be passionate in worship for the One who gave everything He had. Who laid down His life as a bride price, so that we may know the extent of the love He has for each one of us.

'That day will bring about the destruction of the heavens by fire, and the elements will melt in the heat. But in keeping with his promise we are looking forward to a new heaven and a new earth, the home of righteousness.' 2 Peter 3:12b-3

For us the 'Day of the Lord', as it is called throughout scripture will be like no other. The heavens will disappear and the earth will be laid bare, but it will also be the day when our earthly troubles will disappear too. Our Bridegroom is coming to 'steal us away'. He is coming to take His betrothed bride to His Father's house ready for the final stage of the wedding, and the wedding supper of the Lamb.

'Selah'

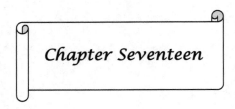

Chapter Seventeen

The Bridal Garments

Having 'stolen' his bride the wedding party would return with the groom and his companions to his father's house. There the bride would be finely dressed for her husband ready for the final ceremony, and she would be crowned.

In the book of Ezekiel there is written down in allegorical form, which is like an Old Testament parable, an amazing description of what our bride could have been dressed in if she was from, or married into a wealthy family.

'I clothed you with an embroidered dress and put leather sandals on you. I *dressed* you in fine linen and covered you with costly garments. I adorned you with jewellery: I put bracelets on your arms and a necklace around your neck, and I put a ring on your nose, ear-rings on your ears and a beautiful *crown* on your head. So you were adorned with gold and silver; your clothes were of *fine linen* and costly fabric and embroidered cloth.' Ezekiel 16:10-13a

Wow! That conjures up an amazing image of how beautiful a wealthy bride could look. Just think, we are marrying the wealthiest Bridegroom that's ever been. He even owns 'the cattle on a thousand hills!' Psalm 50:10

'For the wedding of the Lamb has come, and his *bride* has made herself ready. *Fine linen*, bright and clean was given her *to wear*. (Fine linen stands for the righteous acts of the saints.)' Revelation 19:7b-8

'... prepared as a bride beautifully *dressed* for her husband' Rev 21:2b

Clothes and especially cloaks or robes, in biblical times denoted status. In the Old Testament we read that Esther's uncle Mordecai was given King Xerxes' robe to wear for a day to show the people that he was being honoured by the king. This robe elevated his status and displayed the high regard the king had for him to the people of the city (see Esther 6:11). Then in the book of Job we read that Job tore his robe, as well as put ashes on his head, to signify the grief he felt at the death of his children (see Job 1:20). To tear ones clothes was, and still is in some places today, a sign of mourning. An alteration in what was worn often showed that someone's status had changed. In Job's case it wasn't just his grief that was displayed in the tearing of his clothing.

All his descendants were gone and children, especially sons were considered as being like riches to a father. So his torn clothes showed his reduced status in the 'poverty' of losing everything he owned, as well as all his whole family apart from his wife.

In the New Testament we read in Luke 15:22 that when the prodigal son returned home, his father said, 'Bring the best robe and put it on him.' The son's old clothes may have been underneath the robe for a while, until he had time to change out of them. But the moment the robe was put around him was the moment that denoted his status had changed. The robe, described as being the best, showed that he was no longer a hired hand he was now a son of the father's household once more.

However, one of the clearest confirmations of the importance of clothing, especially robes or cloaks, is in chapter ten of Mark's gospel. Here we read about blind Bartimaeus, who was sitting by the road begging when Jesus was passing by. When he heard that Jesus was there, he cried out saying "Jesus, Son of David, have mercy on me!" The people told him, no warned him, to be quiet, probably because he was just a penniless blind beggar. But instead of being quiet he cried out even more! Jesus hearing his cries, stopped and commanded the people to tell Bartimaeus to come to Him. Being blind, you'd think that Jesus would have gone to Bartimaeus rather than the other way round, but instead He called for Bartimaeus to come to Him. Maybe the reason for this is linked to the significance of clothing. Because the next thing we are told about Bartimaeus is - 'Throwing his cloak aside, he jumped to his feet and came to Jesus' (Mark 10:50).

In our day people have white sticks to tell others around them that they are visually impaired. In those days, it was their distinctive outer cloak that told people that this person was blind. In throwing aside his cloak, Bartimaeus was making a statement of faith - 'I'm not going to need this cloak anymore because Jesus is going to heal me!' In allowing Bartimaeus to go to Him, Jesus gave him the opportunity to respond in such a clear and significant way. Because Jesus didn't even touch Bartimaeus or his eyes; He just asked him what he wanted. Then Jesus told him, "Your faith has healed you", and it had - Bartimaeus could now see!

'For he has clothed me with garments of salvation and arrayed me in a robe of righteousness, as a bridegroom adorns his head like a priest, and as a bride adorns herself with her jewels.' Isaiah 61:10

In Exodus 28 we read that the high priests wore special clothing that had been made for them according to God's instructions. Jesus as our Bridegroom adorns His head like a priest because He is - our High Priest. It tells us that clearly in Hebrews 4:14 '... we have a great high priest who has gone through the heavens, Jesus the Son of God'

When we accepted the price that Jesus paid for our salvation, repented of our sins and accepted Him as our personal Saviour, we were also given special clothing to wear. Although it may not be visible to the human eye, we are told in Isaiah 61:10 that we have been given a robe of righteousness. This robe befits our new position of being a child of God; and it also gives us the status of being a priest unto our God; a priest who is permitted to enter into His presence.

'He who overcomes will, like them be *dressed* in white. I will never blot out his name from the book of life, but will acknowledge his name before my Father and his angels.' Revelation 3:5

If we could see with our human eyes the spiritual clothing that we are wearing right now we would be amazed. But when Jesus returns what we are wearing now will be replaced by a new white garment, which will be far more splendid than we can ever imagine. The Greek word for white is *leukos*, which means brilliant dazzling white, like the garments of angels and those exalted to the splendour of the heavenly state. At the end of the age when we stand under the heavenly canopy, the heavenly *chuppah*, we will be clothed in a beautiful, brilliant, dazzling bridal garment; and we will be wearing a bridal crown.

'And when the Chief Shepherd appears, you will receive the *crown* of glory that will never fade away.' 1 Peter 5:4

'... he will receive the *crown* of life that God has promised to those who love him' James 1:12b

'Now there is in store for me the *crown* of righteousness 2 Timothy 4:8a

The crown of glory according to Peter's first letter; the crown of life that James speaks of; and the crown of righteousness Paul spoke about to Timothy, is the same word *stephanos*. According to my concordance, the crown is given to the genuine servants of God and Christ; it is a reward of their righteousness. This same word *stephanos* also describes a wreath or a garland that would be given to a victor who achieved success in public games, in order to honour them. The nearest equivalent we have to this is receiving a gold medal in the Olympic Games.

The writer to the Hebrews encouraged his readers not to give up as they run the race of the Christian life. He used an analogy that his readers understood of athletes running in one of the great stadiums that they had it that day, which would have been packed with spectators - 'Therefore since we are surrounded by such a great cloud of witnesses, let us throw off everything that hinders and the sin that so easily entangles, and let us run with perseverance the race marked out for us.' (Hebrews 12:1). The writer knew there was a crown to be won, and wanted his readers to make every effort to keep going despite the hindrances that would trip them up. But this crown isn't just for one winner. It is for all those who 'fix their eyes on Jesus'; all those who keep looking to Him to coach them in their spiritual race. The stories of all those faithful people of Hebrews 11 prefix this chapter, and it's their stories that have been written down to encourage us to run with endurance. They are the spectators, along with the angels in heaven, who are constantly cheering us on.

But before we get our victory crown at the end of the race, or our bridal crown when our Bridegroom returns, there is another crown that we can have now.

'Get wisdom, get understanding; do not forget my words or swerve from them.
Do not forsake wisdom, and she will protect you; love her, and she will watch over you.
Wisdom is supreme; therefore get wisdom. Though it cost all you have, get understanding.
Esteem her, and she will exalt you; embrace her, and she will honour you.
She will set a garland of grace on your head and present you with a *crown* of splendour.' Proverbs 4:5-9

'Selah'

Chapter Eighteen

The Third Stage of the Wedding

The third and final stage of the wedding is called the *Nissuin*. This word means elevation. Through this ceremony the bride and groom were to be elevated, lifted up, to the new status of being man and wife in every way.

While the wedding party was assembling for the *Nissuin*, the groomsmen would get the *chuppah* ready. The prayer shawl would be held in place ready for the couple to come under it once more, where their final vows would be said. During those vows the bride declared her independence from her own family. She declared that from this point on she would come under her husband's care and protection; she accepted that her husband's family was now her family and that his father was now her father. She came out from under the covering and protection of her father; she was no longer a member of her birth family; she was now a member of the groom's family. Through the final vows and these declarations she not only became the wife of the groom, she was also 'adopted' by his father into their family. From that point on his father would treat her just as he would one of his own daughters.

'They will *be his people*, and God himself will be with them and be *their God.*' Revelation 21:3

Have you ever wondered why Jesus only spoke about a man leaving his father and mother and being joined to his wife? (see Mark 10:7) Why He didn't say this was important for both men and women to do? The reason was, because the wives had already done that, both verbally and literally, when they had taken their wedding vows, made their declarations and left home to live with their in-laws!

In Ezra chapter nine the people of Israel were commanded not to take husbands for their daughters, or daughters for their sons, from other nations. To do so would have meant serious consequences for the whole community. A daughter who was given in marriage to someone who wasn't from the Jewish faith would be 'adopted' into a family of idol worshippers and be exposed to idol worship for the rest of her life. If a son married a foreign woman from another nation it would mean that the Jewish family would be adopting an idolatrous daughter-in-law into their family.

In Genesis 26 we read that Esau, Jacob's twin brother, married two foreign wives. The result was devastating for his parents, 'When Esau was forty years old, he married Judith daughter of Beeri the Hittite, and also Basemath daughter of Elon the Hittite. They were a source of grief to Isaac and Rebekah.' (Genesis 26:34-35). His parents obviously didn't have much say about who Esau married because he was forty years old by then. But the consequences of his marriages were so bad that they encouraged Jacob to find a wife from among their relatives - 'Then Rebekah said to Isaac, "I'm disgusted with living because of these Hittite women. If Jacob takes a wife from among the women of this land, from Hittite women like these, my life will not be worth living."' (Genesis 27:46).

Marrying out, as it is called, didn't just affect the son it affected the whole family and their household if they had servants. In fact, because Jewish communities were so close, it would expose everyone to the influence of idolatry. The result of intermarriage with the other nations around them, and the idol worship that had inevitably followed, made Israel vulnerable to their enemies. It had resulted in destruction and the nation being taken captive to Babylon. Now that they had returned to the land to rebuild the temple of the LORD and the city of Jerusalem, Ezra cautioned them strongly not to repeat their previous mistakes - 'Now therefore, do not give your daughters in marriage to their sons or take their daughters for your sons.' (Ezra 9:12)

Going back to the story of Ruth we read that Naomi's sons only married Moabite women after their father had died. As a woman under the care and protection of her sons, Naomi would not have had a say in the matter. But I'm sure that Naomi would have spoken wisely to the Moabite daughters-in-law who had been 'adopted' into her family, about the God of Israel whom she loved, as they worked together in the kitchen. Because when her husband died, Ruth turned her back on the idol worship of her own nation and gave her life to staying with Naomi; and she accepted the LORD God of Israel as her own. It's no wonder the following scripture is used so often in our modern day Christian weddings!

'"Don't urge me to leave you or to turn back from you. Where you go I will go, and where you stay I will stay. Your people will be my people and your God my God."' Ruth 1:16

'And by him we cry '*Abba*, Father'. The Spirit himself testifies with our spirit that we are God's children.' Romans 8:15b-16

A daughter-in-law's place in the groom's family was confirmed once the betrothal vows were taken during the *Kiddushin*; and they were finally sealed during the last and final stage of the wedding, the *Nissuin*. The only thing that could change that was if she was found to be pregnant, having committed adultery before or after her betrothal vows; or if, at sometime in the future her husband hardened his heart against her, then he could give her a certificate of divorce and send her away (see Matthew 19:7). This wasn't usual but it could happen.

In the Old Testament book of Hosea, we read of the great lengths our God goes to illustrate that even adultery doesn't stop Him loving His people. The book reveals the negative consequences of unfaithfulness, but also His unconditional love, as He waits for the 'unfaithful wife' to turn back to Him. Throughout the New Testament we are told how much Jesus loves His bride; so much so that 'He gave up His life for her' (Ephesians 5:2). His heart may be grieved at our foolishness sometimes, but it's clear that our Groom's heart could never be hardened against us; and He has made a promise to us saying, 'I will never leave you or forsake you' (Hebrews 13:5 & Deuteronomy 31:6). Then the final proof that He won't divorce us is in Malachi 2:16. It tells us that 'He hates divorce'. I'm sure this is because He hates to see the hurt that broken relationships cause to all those involved. Jesus acknowledged that Moses permitted divorce but only because of men's hard hearts (see Matthew 19:8); but we can be sure it's not something that our Bridegroom would do.

Having committed our lives and made our vows to our Bridegroom here on earth, our heavenly Father treats us and considers us in the same way as a daughter that has committed herself to leave her own father's house and marry into His Family.

'For the Lord himself will come down from heaven...... and the dead in Christ will rise first. After that, we who are still alive and are left will be caught up together with them in the clouds to meet the Lord in the air. And so we will be with the Lord forever. Therefore encourage each other with these words.' 1 Thessalonians 4: 16-18

For now, we have to accept by faith all that scripture tells us with regards to who we are, and how much we are loved and accepted. But one day our *Nissuin*, our elevation will take place, when we are caught up in the clouds; when He comes to take us back to His Father's house for the final stage of our wedding. It is then that we will know in reality, that we truly are one with Him; that His Father is our Father, and we will live with Him forever as part of His Family.

'Selah'

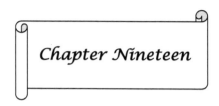

Chapter Nineteen

The Wedding Supper

After the vows and declarations came the final blessings and the final covenant cup would be drunk.

'After taking *the cup*, he gave thanks and said, "Take this and divide it among you. For I tell you I will not drink again of the fruit of the vine *until* the Kingdom of God comes"' Luke 22:17-18

The final ceremony was over, all the stages of the wedding had been completed, and now it was time to celebrate. It was time for the Wedding Supper to begin! This wasn't like our modern day wedding reception, which takes place after the wedding service and is over and done with on the same day. The Wedding Supper was seven days of celebration with food, music and dance. These were times of great rejoicing and enjoyment!

'Then the angel said to me, "Write: Blessed are those who are invited to the wedding supper of the Lamb!"' Revelation 19:9

In John's gospel we read that Jesus performed His first miracle at a wedding in Cana of Galilee. During the wedding supper His mother Mary, drew His attention to the fact that they had run out of wine. This meant there was a real potential for the bridegroom to be embarrassed before the bride's family, and the whole community. So Mary decided to ask Jesus to step in and do something about it. She called the servants and said to them, "Do whatever He tells you."

'Nearby stood six stone water jars, the kind used by the Jews for ceremonial washing, each holding from twenty to thirty gallons.
Jesus said to the servants, "Fill the jars with water," so they filled them to the brim.
Then he told them, "Now draw some out and take it to the master of the banquet."
They did so, and the master of the banquet tasted the water that had been turned into wine. He did not realise where it had come from, though the servants who had drawn the water knew. Then he called the bridegroom aside and said, "Everyone brings out the choice wine first and then the cheaper wine after the guests have had too much to drink; but you have saved the best till now."' John 2:6-10

The emphasis of this parable has always been that the water was turned into wine. But there is more to this miracle than meets the eye. The stone water jars that were used for ceremonial washing were filled to the brim; and each jar could hold around 20-30 gallons of water. Taking an average of 25 gallons, it works out that every jar held approximately 115 litres. Multiply that by six, being the number of jars they filled, and we find that Jesus supplied around 690 litres of wine for the banquet. To put that into the context of a modern day bottle of wine that holds 750ml, it would be fair to say that in this miracle Jesus produced approximately 920 bottles of wine from those jars of water. This wasn't a 'necessary' miracle of healing or provision. But it was a miracle that saved the groom from being embarrassed in front of his bride, her family and all the guests.

This account of the water being turned into wine in John's gospel helps us to understand that the wedding suppers of the Old and New Testament times weren't small, one day affairs. They lasted for seven days and, if the wedding that Mary and Jesus attended is anything to go by, they required a lot of wine. The 690 litres that Jesus supplied was in addition to what had been already drunk! The number seven is considered, in Jewish culture and scripture, to be the number of perfection or completion. For the bride and groom these seven days of the wedding supper certainly marked the completion of all three stages of their wedding.

'I saw the Holy City, the new Jerusalem, coming down out of heaven from God, prepared as a bride beautifully dressed for her husband. And I heard a loud voice from the throne saying, 'Now the dwelling of God is with men, and he will live with them. They will be his people, and God himself will be with them and be their God.' Revelation 21:2-4

The words in the book of Revelation are said to be allegorical in that they are figurative and symbolic. Those who read this book are promised to be blessed, but no-one will fully understand it until it is revealed at the end of time. All we truly need to know is that, as the bride of Christ, the Wedding Supper of the Lamb is the completion of all the stages in our wedding too. But there is one more thing I want to share with you.

'Selah'

Chapter Twenty

The Consummation

When the father told his son that all was ready and it was time for him to go and claim his bride, before he left, the groom would prepare the way for his bride to be welcomed into his home and his family in the traditional way.

The traditional way to show any guest that they were welcome to someone's home was for the host to pour out the blood of an animal or bird into a basin that was permanently set into the threshold of his house. The more important the guest was, the more costly the animal would be that was offered in this way. When the guest stepped over that threshold, he entered not just into the host's home he entered into a covenant with the host that was very powerful and very strong. This covenant meant the host and the guest would honour and respect each other and the family, and would never do them any harm. The guest would be treated as if he was part of the family for as long as he remained under the family's roof. This was called a threshold covenant.

This covenant not only applied to guests. When a son married he would pour out the blood of the most expensive animal or bird that he could afford, in the threshold of his father's house ready for when he returned with his new bride. The poured out blood confirmed and made legal the covenant she was about to enter into, not just with her groom, but with his whole family.

Having prepared the threshold in this way, when the final ceremony, the *Nissuin*, was complete, the groom would then pick up his bride in his arms and he would carry her over the threshold, over the blood that was poured out in the threshold of his father's house!

I think it's true to say that most of us have seen a groom carry his bride over the threshold of their home whether personally, on the television or when watching a film. Many of us will ourselves have been carried over the threshold by our husbands. I certainly was on our wedding night, to the amusement of a group of boys who happened to be watching from across the street! But most of us don't realise that this tradition of being carried over the threshold began long ago and it originates from the threshold covenant.

The threshold covenant is the reason why a thief would never enter through the door to steal from someone, 'Most assuredly, I say to you, he who does not enter the sheepfold by the door, but climbs up some other way, the same is a thief and a robber.' (John 10:1). Because to step over the threshold of a doorway in order to steal or do someone harm, meant that the thief would become a covenant breaker - and as such he would bring a curse upon his life! Everyone knew this and it is why they could safely leave their homes unlocked whenever they went out.

The threshold covenant was behind the words of Jesus when he told the people in John 10:9 - "I am the *door*. If anyone *enters* by me, he will be saved, and will go in and out and find pasture." It was also behind what He said in John 14:6 - "I am the way and the truth and the life. No one comes to the Father except *through* me." These are cultural references to the threshold covenant; and the full meaning behind them have been hidden to those of us brought up in other cultures and in another age.

The scripture - "Behold, I stand at the door and knock" (Revelation 3:20) is a request for us to open the door to Him so that He can come in to our 'house'. If we do that and open the door of our life to Him, then it can be said that we have 'Christ in us'. Therefore, if we in that sense are a house, then Jesus is also a 'house'. In fact He referred to His body in John 2:19 & 21 as a Temple.

When Jesus died He poured out His blood at the threshold of His 'house'. Then after we His bride had taken our vows and made our declarations of commitment to Him, our Bridegroom picked us up in His arms and carried us over His poured out blood and into His 'house' - into Christ! What a wonderful picture! It shows us that we are both 'in Christ' and we have 'Christ in us'!

'And God raised us up with Christ and seated us with him in the heavenly realms *in Christ* Jesus' Ephesians 2:6

But how can that be? We are still waiting for our Bridegroom to come for us for the final stage of the wedding, which will take place under the heavenly canopy, the heavenly *chuppah,* at the end of the age! The answer is that our spirit has already been carried over the threshold of His Father's house; over His poured out blood. The rest will take place when He comes back with the angelic host, just as we have been promised.

As the groom carried his bride over the blood that had been poured out in the threshold, he carried her into a covenantal agreement that was very powerful and very strong. This covenant bonded her to his family, and it signified the groom's sincerity and intent. The animal or bird was accepted as a substitute for his life; and the poured out blood said to his new bride, in a way that was more graphic than mere words could ever say - "I lay my life down for you dear wife. This is how much I love you!"

'Husbands, love your wives, just as Christ loved the church and gave himself up for her.' Ephesians 5:25

The moment the groom's right foot touched the ground on the other side of the threshold - his bride became part of his family. All that was his was now hers; and all that belonged to his family was now hers, forever. His father became her father. She came under their roof and under their protection. Then on their wedding night, as the marriage was consummated, and the bride poured out the blood of her virginity at her personal threshold, the marriage covenant was finally sealed - made legal by the shedding of blood!

They had completed all the stages of the wedding that were required. What was initiated in the arrangement stage of the wedding all those years before had finally come to pass!

'I am My Beloved's and He is Mine'

'... he who is joined to the Lord is one spirit with him' 1 Corinthians 6:17 (NKJV)

Christ is in us by His Holy Spirit, and we are in Christ spiritually, even though our body is still here on earth. Therefore we are part of His family now. All that is His is ours; and all that belongs to His family is ours. His Father is our Father; and we have come under His roof and under His protection.

One day when His Father says so, when all is ready, our Bridegroom will come and we will be clothed with dazzling white garments and wear a crown. We will attend the Wedding Supper of the Lamb with Him and fulfil the final stage of the wedding. The New Covenant, our marriage covenant, which was arranged by the Father through the Matchmaker, the Holy Spirit and made legal by the shedding of Jesus' blood all those years before, will finally come to pass in all its fullness.

In the meantime dear friends, if you have said "Yes" to the Matchmaker, the Holy Spirit, and committed your life to Him, remember you have been chosen by the Father to marry His Son. You have taken your vows to be His bride and you are betrothed to your Groom and those betrothal vows are binding. It would need Him to present you with a contract of divorce to separate you from Him. But He won't, because His heart is not hard, it is full of love for you, He has laid down His life for you. One day we will see Him face to Face, but 'Only the Father knows' when that will be.

As surely as the betrothed couple were joined to each other - even though they lived apart, our spirit is one with our Bridegroom's Spirit; and because of that we are seated with Him in heavenly places right now. Then when the Father says to our Groom, *"All is ready; now is the time. You may go and claim Your bride"*, we will take our final vows and our oneness with Him will be complete.

'Selah'

'How To Pray When
He Doesn't Believe'
by Mo Tizzard

"It's God or me!"

That was the ultimatum Mo faced when she told her husband she had become a Christian. It was the beginning of a time of great pressure and discord in their marriage, but also a time of incredible learning about how to pray and live with her husband under the guidance of the Lord.

'How To Pray When He Doesn't Believe' tells Mo's story chapter by chapter; and each of those chapters are accompanied by principles of prayer and scriptural teaching. The book offers authentic encouragement to every woman who is married to an unbeliever. Mo speaks into the real issues, in practical ways, as only someone who has 'walked the walk' can do.

The prayers and insights in this book are designed to be helpful, not only for those with unsaved husbands, but for anyone praying for unsaved loved ones or friends; and many have testified to how this book has encouraged them in praying for their 'prodigals' to 'come home'.

Because it addresses a need that affects believers in any nation, Mo's book has been translated by foreign publishers in France, The Czech Republic, Korea and Russia; as well as being published in the USA.

"Mo has written a fascinating and engrossing story of a spiritual drama that will hold your interest to the last page. Her honest and realistic portrayal of the facts interspersed with helpful Biblical teaching and concepts will be of great value to those who find themselves in a similar situation. A highly readable book, which will help all those with loved ones who are not yet Christians."

Jeanette Barwick
Head of Women's Ministry, CWR
(Crusade for World Revival)

"Mo documents her journey of faith detailing how she overcame each obstacle. She writes about the value of simple attitude changes, learning when to keep silent and a discovery of how to pray strategically – culminating in the salvation of her husband. This sensitive and candid account will inspire any women in a similar position, to a new surge of faith."

Paula Cummings
Communications Manager
The London Institute for Contemporary Christianity

Please visit Mo's website - www.motizzard.com for more information on her books.